OUR
# ABANDONED
CHILDREN

# OUR
# ABANDONED
## CHILDREN

History of the **Child Welfare System**

# DR. RON HUBER

iUniverse LLC
Bloomington

# OUR ABANDONED CHILDREN
## History of the Child Welfare System

iUniverse books may be ordered through booksellers or by contacting:

iUniverse LLC
1663 Liberty Drive
Bloomington, IN 47403
www.iuniverse.com
1-800-Authors (1-800-288-4677)

ISBN: 978-1-4759-9974-7 (sc)
ISBN: 978-1-4759-9976-1 (hc)
ISBN: 978-1-4759-9975-4 (ebk)

Library of Congress Control Number: 2013913174

Printed in the United States of America

iUniverse rev. date: 07/19/2013

# Preface

Growing up in the foster care system of Chicago, Illinois, in the 1940s, with vivid images still swirling around inside his racing mind, he conjures up unspeakable sadness—the dreaded, tragic realities of a broken system that was supposed to assist the kids with no other place on this planet to go to grow up and thrive But instead, it failed kids like Ronnie.

The story highlights Ronnie's own personal struggles with social acceptance and an introverted personality borne of repeated criticism and harshness. But like any good ""Cinderonnie" story, the triumph quells the storm when the warmth of one particular family fills the long-standing ache and encompasses Ronnie, teaching him what being loved is all about and showing us all that the power of love can take us to heights that our beginnings never would have forecast.

# Chapter 1

The scope and breadth of the cruelty I suffered as I was being carted from one foster home to the next after I was abandoned by my impoverished, troubled, uncaring alcoholic mother and father and raised by couples who were ill equipped to accommodate the emotional needs of a child was so staggering that the hurt never went away, nor did the secrets I still keep inside my emotional prison. On this day—my very first day at school—it cut like a bare bodkin deep into my flesh. The humiliation of it all struck like a stake through my heart as I stood embarrassed in the middle of the classroom and the echo of children's laughter rang like a moving freight train in my ears. I was living in my second foster home, and my initial excitement about the first day of school quickly diminished. My face felt flush, and my tongue would not work. The teacher, after what seemed like forever, allowed me to sit down. But the damage had already been done; being branded as stupid by my peers for not knowing my own mother's name burned an indelible scar on my heart. What they never knew was that my ignorance of who my mother wasn't on account of a faulty memory or being some mentally retarded misfit. I didn't know my mother's name because I had never gotten a chance to ask. Her name was Helen Mae Somerville, but to Vic, Ralph Jr., and me, she was a ghost, a shadow. The local bar saw more of her than we did. It was very clear that this strange woman did not want us. A letter written by the caseworker of the Peoria Red Cross dated November 10, 1948, read,

> Mrs. Ralph Somerville had come to the Peoria Red Cross office for advice and help in solving her problems regarding family finances and care for her three children, ages 4 years, 3 years and 10 months, all boys. Mr. Somerville worked on a boat earning $75 every two weeks. They had been living in

a seven room house in Bureau, Illinois, paying $75 a month rent and $30 a month for electricity. The house did not heat properly and the landlord refused to make the necessary improvements. The family had many debts and Mrs. Somerville was embarrassed to go into stores in Bureau. Mr. Somerville was a veteran, and it was thought by the Peoria Red Cross Worker that the family would be eligible for planning on the Illinois Soldiers and Sailors Children's School (I.S.S.C.S.) program. The mother was said to be quite upset by the whole situation and became emotional during the interview in Peoria. The mother seemed to want to place her children temporarily until the family could get along financially. No relative could or was willing to help the family.

And in a letter dated November 18, the caseworker expressed further concern over the family's emergency situation.

The children were sleeping on the floor in a house that had no heat, and it is necessary that they get out of the house. All of the children are sick with colds and Mrs. Somerville was so sick the Red Cross sent her to the doctor. The doctor reported afterwards that Mrs. Somerville needed rest and that she was not strong enough at this time to work, although the mother said she has a job in Joliet. As for Ron, the records show his mother describes him as "having no illnesses." The only difference she has noticed about Ronald from the other children is the fact that he drags one of his legs from running. As yet she has never taken him to the doctor to find out what was wrong with it. She describes Ronald as a very nervous child.

My grandfather was our primary caretaker. Unfortunately, he was an alcoholic as well and only looked in on us from time to time. On a good day, when he was sober, he would bring us something to eat. If he was feeling especially kind, he would take the extra time to clean our bodies of the horrible stench that developed from sitting in our own excrement for several days. I imagine, though, that it was more for his personal comfort rather than a result of any sympathy he had for us. Our pained whimpers were ignored as he roughly raked soap and water over our little bodies, irritating the sores that had developed on our tender backsides. Then he dressed us in clothes that he'd bought from the Salvation Army. They weren't quite as dirty as the ones we'd taken off, so it was a bit of an improvement. After a peanut butter and jelly sandwich and a glass of water, our moment in the spotlight would be over. With so much attention having been doted on us at once, it would often be several days before we saw him or ate again. The rats in the building lived better than we did. My father, Ralph Wesley Somerville, worked for Federal Barge Lines on a boat named the *Montgomery* over in Chicago. He was often gone for weeks at a time, sending his paychecks home without any thought as to how they were spent. I'm sure he had to know that my mother and grandfather were drinking them up. Perhaps he didn't care, but I am more inclined to believe he forgot we were there. He stayed gone so long that he barely noticed us when he was at home.

Because of our parents' absence, we spent most of our days amusing ourselves on the cold and dirty linoleum floor in the kitchen. Vic and I, ages four and three, didn't talk much but developed our own method of communication. The two of us did our best to keep our younger brother, Ralph Jr., content. We knew he was just as hungry as we were, but he was usually too weak to cry even if he was upset. In the Red Cross entry from November 30, 1948, Mrs. Booth described our mother as an irresponsible person who was completely uninterested in her children and thoroughly inadequate as a mother. The housekeeping standards were poor; she said we children were as dirty and poorly clothed as one could imagine. Apparently, there was very little for us to eat. All three of us were like little animals over our food after the placements were made.

Those days were a dismal existence for us, but then life changed on one blisteringly cold November day in 1948. It was nearly noon, but the sky was dark and menacing. The wind outside was biting, and it swirled threateningly against the window of our front room, making a loud whirring sound. A battered heater stood in the corner of the room, sputtering and creaking, but it failed to emit any significant warmth. We could see our breath float across the room like puffs of clouds. According to the records of the Peoria Red Cross, Mom stated that she and our dad wanted very badly to be able to provide a good home for us. But she added that because of a change in plans in the Bureau, they were not able to. She felt that putting us in the ISSCS program had been in our best interest until she and Dad could get established and get a home for us, at which time she would want to have us back. The record said,

> Mrs. Somerville was rather emotional about the fact that the Red Cross throughout their contact with her implied neglect of her children and said that was because of this the state would come and take her children away. She emphasized the fact that this was only a temporary arrangement until she and her husband were ready to move into their new home and one of them could be home. Mrs. Somerville put no length of time to this proposition.

It was one of those rare days that my mother was at home. Each of us vied for her attention, but she batted us away like flies. When we begged for something to eat, she turned a deaf ear and looked right through us as if we weren't there. Her stare was glassy. It was the look of someone desperately trying to remain sober but coming precariously close to losing that battle.

Sometime around midafternoon, a large black sedan slowed to a stop in front of our house. Curious, we perched on the worn sofa and looked out through the living room window. We watched as two husky-looking women emerged and struggled purposely against the wind toward our front door. We rushed to tell my mother but found that she was also watching from behind a curtain in the other room. When the ladies reached the walkway, she rushed to the door and let them in.

The room seemed to disappear when they stepped inside. Their faces were fixed in scowls, and they didn't say a word. They looked in our direction and then followed my mother into the kitchen. I felt a chill that had nothing to do with the cold.

Once inside the kitchen, they spoke in hushed tones. Occasionally, someone's voice would rise slightly and cause us to watch the door anxiously. Vic and I were too young to consider eavesdropping and probably would not have comprehended the deal that was being made behind the door anyway. They all returned to the front room a few minutes later. The room remained quiet, and I shifted uncomfortably. I was so nervous; suddenly, I felt warm wetness trickling down my leg. Embarrassed, I tried to cover the wet spot. Everyone turned in my direction. My mother stared through me and made no move to clean me up. Both women frowned at me and then shot my mother an irritated glare.

Then, to my surprise, the smaller of the two women marched over to the crib where little Ralph was sleeping. She stared down at him for a moment and then turned and nodded at my mother. Grabbing a blanket that hung across the railing, she wrapped him tightly. She placed a tattered hat on his head, picked him up and headed toward the front door without saying a word.

Vic and I whirled around in my mother's direction, expecting her to protest, but she remained mute. Her gaze was fixed on the floor. Confused, I ran to the window and watched as the woman continued to walk down the sidewalk to the car, carrying my brother in her arms.

I'd been so preoccupied with Ralph's fate that I gave no thought to what was about to happen to Vic and me. A commotion stirred up behind me and regained my attention—I'd completely forgotten about the other woman in the room. To my dismay, I turned to find her tugging insistently at Vic's arm. He cried and squirmed desperately, trying to resist. I looked from the scene before me to my mother, who still had not moved. It seemed as though her feet were glued to the floorboard. What was going on? I spun back around in my brother's direction just in time to see this hulking woman crouch down to his eye level and glare menacingly into his face.

"If you don't shut up right this second, I'll smack the daylights out of you!"

The sharpness of her tone stopped Vic midway. The woman straightened back up, yanked his arm, and motioned for me to follow them. My eyes were as wide as saucers, but I didn't say anything. Any ideas I may have had about disobeying faded quickly after hearing her threaten my brother. My eyes welled up with tears, which fell silently down my cheeks. I hung my head and began to walk slowly behind them down the sidewalk to the car. The huge car door loomed ominously before me. With one final gust of hope, I glanced back toward the front door, only to be chilled by the coldness of my mother's indifference. Reluctantly, I climbed inside. A feeling of hopelessness and abandon swept through me as the car door closed us inside, and our front door disappeared from sight.

We rode through the city in silence except for Ralph's occasional squeals from the front seat. Our stomachs grumbled loudly and drew disapproving frowns from the woman who had finally identified herself as Mrs. Booth. Vic and I tapped each other, pointing and straining to look out of the window. As we continued along the highway, we watched the scenery change from rural fields to bustling city streets. It was early evening when we pulled up in front of Covenant Children's Home.

Covenant Children's Home was a huge, two-story, beige brick establishment that stood on the corner of a middle-class neighborhood. The cloudy sky cast a gloomy shadow over the building, giving it an uninviting appearance. When Mrs. Booth opened the door and instructed us to get out, I got a sinking feeling in my stomach. What was this place? More importantly, why were we here? The Peoria Red Cross documents tell the story.

> The two older Somerville children were placed at the Covenant Children's home on 11-19-48 and baby Ralph Somerville wad placed in the home of Mr. and Mrs. Johnson on the same date. It had been arranged by Mrs. Booth that the two older children should go to the Covenant Children's Home while Baby Ralph could be taken care of temporarily by a family with whom the mother has made arrangements at [the] Bureau [of] Illinois.

Reluctantly, we got out and peered up the stairs leading to the strange building. Mrs. Johnson, the smaller woman, stayed in the car holding Ralph Jr., while Mrs. Booth walked quickly toward the steps, grumbling over her shoulder for us to come along. She never noticed that we had not moved from our spots on the sidewalk. When she reached the top step, the front door opened, and a man emerged. He spoke briefly to Mrs. Booth and then looked down at us. Reverend Videen was a tall, thin, friendly-looking man. He smiled warmly and motioned for us to come closer. It was the first inviting look we'd seen in quite some time. Vic rushed toward the stairs. I was right behind him, but before I could reach the first step, I let out a faint squeal, and my poor malnourished body collapsed. Vic rushed back to my side but was unable to be of much help. He was just as frail as I was. Upon seeing my difficulty, Reverend Videen came down, scooped me up in his arms, and carried me inside.

A small hallway and several flights of stairs later, we entered a room filled with several round tables covered with red and white tablecloths. The delicious smell of freshly baked cookies wafted in from the kitchen, and my stomach pitched hungrily. The reverend took us to a nearby sink and helped us wash our grimy hands before seating us at one of the tables. We sat there expectantly, not saying a word. Minutes, which seemed like hours, later, a smiling, heavyset woman wearing an apron came out of the kitchen and placed two plates of steaming food in front of us. Both Vic and I sat there, momentarily stunned. Hot food was a luxury that we had not had on a frequent basis. The aroma of the hot turkey and mashed potatoes was intoxicating. I looked anxiously at Reverend Videen. Were we supposed to eat this? Was it okay?

"Aren't you hungry?" he asked with a puzzled expression. I nodded vigorously, unable to make a sound.

"Please," he urged softly, "eat up, boys."

No further prompting was necessary. Hovering protectively over our plates, Vic and I immediately began shoveling food into our mouths with our hands. The hot potatoes and gravy burned my tiny fingers, but I barely noticed as I continued to rush scoop after scoop into my mouth. It couldn't have been more than five minutes before the cook returned from the kitchen with a small basket of rolls. Her eyes widened in amazement at our nearly clean plates. She glanced at Reverend Videen, who shook his head sadly. After placing the basket down on the table, she disappeared into the kitchen once more, returning with two glasses of cold milk. By that time, we'd eaten everything that had been placed before us. I licked my gravy-covered lips and fingers. My stomach groaned loudly for more, but for the time being, that was all we would get.

Mrs. Porter was a petite woman with graying hair and a pleasant smile. Reverend Videen introduced us to her after dinner. Her hand was warm and soft, and my small one felt good inside of it. She led us into a bathroom upstairs and deposited us into a warm tub. I couldn't remember the last time I'd been completely immersed in water and certainly had not seen bubbles in years. Mrs. Porter showed us how to put them in our palms and blow them at each other. We laughed as the white foam landed on our noses and foreheads. Her touch was gentle as she soaped and rinsed us off. The color of the water when we emerged was a dingy gray.

Clad in warm pajamas, we padded down the hall behind Mrs. Porter to a large room with many twin beds filled with little boys who were already sleeping. She pointed to two empty beds and turned back the covers on each bed. We slid happily into the clean, sweet-smelling sheets. My face sunk into the big, fluffy pillow, and I sighed deeply. Vic fell asleep instantly. Before I drifted off, I thought that if this was only a dream, I didn't ever want to wake up.

# Chapter 2

In a letter to the child welfare office in Rockford, Illinois, Mr. Videen wrote the following letter dated February 9, 1949.

> Your letter of the 28th was received last week. I believe that plans for the future of the Somerville children should be carefully considered. We believe this because of the condition of the children when we received them and also because of the report on the home from which they came, which was given to us by the Red Cross through Mrs. Booth. When we received the children, they were undernourished and weak. The younger of the two is just getting to the place where he can walk up a flight of stairs. Neither of them had any training, and we had to resort to diapers nor rubber pants as soon as they were received. They had to be taught how to eat and how to respect property. When the parents came to visit them, Ronald, the younger child, would have nothing to do with them. He did not remember them, and he seems to be afraid of strangers. Victor responded when they offered him some playthings and spent considerable time with them. I am not sure if he recognized them or just responded to their offer of gifts. After they were gone, he asked for them no more. If the children return to their parents and receive the same treatment they had before, we would consider it very unfortunate for the boys. Everyone here loves Ronald—he is so sweet—and Victor has many friends among the children. We hope the children can find a good home.

As days turned into weeks, I stopped worrying that someone was going to take us away from the home. Shortly after our arrival, a doctor examined us. I was diagnosed with a severe case of rickets, stemming from the malnutrition of my past. Having breakfast, lunch, and dinner on a regular basis helped to strengthen my body. I welcomed each trip to the cafeteria and in those first few days gorged myself every chance I could. Several volunteers spent their time at Covenant working with the children. Despite their friendly demeanor, Vic and I were initially very withdrawn. Over time, their constant attention and encouragement managed to forge a crack in the shell that I'd been enveloped in. Soon, I was racing around the playground with all the other children and enjoying it very much.

Lessons became a part of the daily routine as well. Before going to the children's home, the ABC's had been like a foreign language to us. I had difficulty forming words and often became frustrated, opting not to talk at all. Reverend Videen was very concerned about our social and academic development, and he spent a lot of time visiting with us. He was a kind and patient man.

We were being shown so much encouragement and love that we began to flourish. The friendships that we made with the other children and the staff chased away the pain of hunger and loneliness. It soon became a distant memory.

December brought a beautiful blanket of snow to the city. Snow was something that I had previously only watched from our window because our clothes were never warm enough to allow us to play outside in it. But this year was different. Dressed in thick woolen coats, hats, gloves, and earmuffs, we rolled around with the other kids, making snowmen and snow angels. A snowball fight started after a while. The first time I was hit, it surprised me. The cold ice hit my coat and spattered up onto my face. The blast of air was exciting, and I hurriedly scooped up some snow and packed it into a ball. When I hurled it in the direction of one of the boys we were playing with, it landed perfectly. Soon after, I became known for my terrific aim, and when teams were chosen, I was one of the first ones picked. To have friends was a wonderful feeling, and I looked forward to each opportunity to go outside.

Before we knew it, Christmas was just a few days away. We watched, rapt with amazement, at the hustling and bustling that was going on. The staff invited us to help put up the decorations. The beautiful gold, green, and red garland felt silky in my hand and tickled my cheek as I helped wrap it around the branches of the tree. Vic and I had never had a Christmas tree, so decorating one was a new experience. The balls showed our reflections. We all looked into them, making funny faces, laughing, and eating more popcorn than we strung on the tree.

The hypnotic smell of freshly baked cookies filled the air and tempted our noses while we waited impatiently to get our hands on them. When they were finally ready, we sat down on the floor and sang Christmas carols in between bites of warm cookies and drinks of cider.

As it got closer and closer to Christmas, we watched the other children leave with their parents to spend Christmas Day together. It seemed strange to us that their parents were taking them home only to bring them back after Christmas. Nevertheless, the kids bounced around eagerly, waiting to be picked up. Vic and I also waited. I wasn't sure if I wanted to see my mom and dad or not. Perhaps if they came they would want to take us home too. That was not a thought I relished. However, I did want to see little Ralph. We hadn't seen him since the day we arrived at the home. I often went to sleep wondering if he was having as much fun as us.

When we went downstairs on Christmas morning, our mouths dropped open. Boxes of all shapes and sizes, wrapped in beautiful, shiny paper, sat around the tree. The staff had purposely kept the presents hidden to keep us from shaking them, trying to figure out what they were.

There was a present for each child who had remained behind. I stood staring at the beautiful paper for several seconds, not wanting to tear it. I had a hard time believing it was for me.

Finally, I slid my finger into a seam and ripped the package open. Vic looked over my shoulder anxiously. He'd already torn into his present and was eager to see what I'd gotten.

I lifted the lid of the box. Inside was a knit sweater similar to the one Vic had received. Also inside was a bag of shiny marbles and some candy canes.

I smiled and said, "Thank you." Then we raced outside to play.

# Chapter 3

January was blisteringly cold. We'd come inside after rolling around in freshly fallen snow. My cheeks would be red and stinging as the warmth of the auditorium heated them. I pulled off my mittens and wiggled my fingers.

"Hurry up," said Jerry, one of my playmates. We were late for a music class, one of my favorites. There was something about singing that made me forget all about where I was. I hung up my things hurriedly and ran behind Jerry down the hallway. Just as I turned the corner, I stumbled into Mrs. Porter.

"S-s-sorry," I stuttered. I hung my head, waiting for her to chastise me about running indoors.

"I was just coming to get you, Ronnie. Come with me." My eyes widened with surprise. Why was she looking for me? Where were we going? I followed her down the hallway, up the stairs, and into the auditorium. It was empty, and Mrs. Porter's shoes echoed as they clicked across the hardwood floor.

There was a group of chairs arranged in a far corner. When we reached them, she instructed me to sit down. "Am I in trouble?" I asked nervously. Mrs. Porter hadn't said a word since we'd started walking, and I was afraid that I had done something I wasn't supposed to. I wished Vic was there, but he was in a class somewhere.

Mrs. Porter stopped rearranging the chairs and chuckled as she looked down at me. "No, Ronnie, you are not in trouble. There's someone who wants to see you."

My heart leapt with anticipation. Was someone really going to take us home? Wait—what about Vic? Just as quickly, my spirits sank. I couldn't imagine going anywhere without my brother. My eyes began to water as I looked around. I wanted to take off running but had nowhere to go. "Now what are you crying for?"

I almost jumped out of my seat. Reverend Videen had walked up behind me and placed his hand on my shoulder. "I want to see my brother," I cried.

"What's wrong, Ronnie?" Vic asked as he came running into the auditorium at full speed. He slid slightly as he came to a stop in front of me. His face was creased with concern. "Was somebody picking on you?"

Suddenly, I felt silly with all three of them looking at me. I wiped away the tears with the back of my hand and sniffled loudly. "No, I'm fine," I answered quietly. Mrs. Porter handed me a tissue, and I blew my nose. The sound of clicking made me look up again. There was a man and a woman hurrying across the hardwood floor. It was my mother and father.

"Mother!" Vic bolted from the chair next to me and ran in their direction. My mother rushed to meet him. He crashed into her arms, and she hugged him tightly. I watched with a puzzled expression. I couldn't remember my mother ever being that affectionate before. Had something changed? My father walked over and stood awkwardly in front of me holding two bulky packages. I looked up at him. His face was unshaven and worn looking. His eyes were expressionless, and they made me shiver slightly. He was looking at me as if he didn't know who I was. I wanted to crawl under the seat, but by that time my mother had come over. She was still hugging on Vic when she reached down to me. I cringed slightly at her touch; I wasn't sure if I wanted her to hug me or not. Part of me wanted them both to go away and never come back, but the other part of me wanted to race upstairs, pack my few belongings, and go home. My need for affection won the battle, and I stood under the warmth of her embrace, hoping that maybe something was different. Maybe we really were going home.

"Just look at the two of you!" my mother gushed as she took a step back and gave Vic and me the once over. She was beaming as if we'd only been away at summer camp. "Got something for you," she cooed, reaching and taking the packages from my father. She thrust the two odd-shaped packages at us and continued to smile nervously down at us. Vic grabbed his anxiously and began tearing off the paper. I hesitated and looked up at my mother carefully. She looked thinner than I remembered. Her face seemed to have more lines in it. Though the smile was still fixated on her face, she seemed to lose interest in us after handing us the presents. Her foot tapped impatiently as she watched Vic open his gift. I wanted to hug her again to see if she really was glad to see us, but she didn't look my way again, and she kept her arms folded. My attention was diverted by Vic's squeal; he'd gotten a shiny red fire truck. He plopped down on the floor and rolled it around, making siren noises.

"Open yours, Ronnie! Hurry up!" he said. I traced around the face of the Santa Claus on my wrapping paper and looked around. I didn't really want to open the present. What I wanted was for my mother and father to sit down. I wanted someone to tell me that we were going home now. Even though things at the home had been going well, I wanted Mama and Daddy to tuck me in at night.

But instead, they stood in front of us. My mother's initial display of maternal affection seemed to have swept out in the same gust that she'd rushed in with. Now she appeared antsy and ready to go.

"Open your gift, Ronnie." My father's voice broke the silence. They were the first words he'd said since he arrived. Suddenly I felt embarrassed. Everybody was watching me. Finally, I tore into the paper with mild enthusiasm. I'd also received a truck. I sat it on the floor in front of me and looked around. My mother and father were engrossed in a conversation with Reverend Videen. They had already put their gloves back on.

"We couldn't come on Christmas," my father explained.

"No money for presents, you know," my mother added.

Reverend Videen nodded absently. He was looking over at us. Vic had barely looked up from his truck, but I was watching the grown-up conversation intently. "Perhaps you'd like to join the boys for lunch," the reverend suggested. "I'm sure the boys would love to show you some of the projects they've been working on. You'll be pleased with the progress they've made." He'd barely been able to finish his sentence before my father began shaking his head.

"We can't stay," my father said.

Any hope that I had about leaving that day that had not already been squashed was finally extinguished. The fact that our parents did not want us had just been made crystal clear. Even Vic stopped what he was doing and stared.

Reverend Videen stopped trying to persuade them. My mother came over, patted us each on the head, and murmured for us to "be good." My father looked at us distantly, and then they were gone. With crushed feelings, I got up, walked over to the big window, and looked outside. I watched as they hurried down the walkway, got into an old, beat-up looking car, and drove away.

Mrs. Porter had silently returned. She reached for my hand and pulled me away from the window. The tears streamed down my face as she hugged both Vic and me. She held us for a long time before taking us over to the cafeteria for lunch.

Neither Vic nor I ate very much during lunch or dinner. I couldn't stop myself from thinking about the other children who had gone home with their parents during Christmas. I wondered what was so different about Vic and me that made our parents not want to take us with them. What was so bad about us that nobody had come for us yet? I cried myself to sleep thinking that we'd never leave the home, and for the first time in a long time, I wanted to be anywhere but there.

Red Cross entry dated November 30, 1945:

> Mrs. Booth gave some information about the way the Somerville family in a most critical [and] most condemning way. She did not seem to have an interest in or sincere sympathy for the mother of these children and showed little understanding of a child's particular needs. Objectively Victor and Ronnie's not having been toilet trained at the time of placement when they were 3 1/2 and 2 1/2 years old respectively is suggestive of problems existing. The parent's attitude regarding problems the children may have presented is not known. But the inferred impression is that they were not able to handle them through a lack of insight and understanding. Many time parents would place their children on the toilet for hours, hoping they would learn to use the toilet instead of their diapers In my case. The effort was unrewarding. I just fell asleep.

# Chapter 4

It was especially difficult to bounce back from the disappointment of my parents' visit. Initially, I became pretty despondent, falling back in my lessons and not wanting to play with the other kids. But as time passed, I slowly returned to my usual self.

Along with the success in our lessons, Vic and I were becoming pretty self-sufficient. For the first time, we had a reason to feel proud of ourselves. We had learned to keep our area clean, along with the other twelve boys in our room. We also learned to fold and put away the clothes we received from donations to Covenant. We were so impressed with our new jeans, T-shirts and shoes that we wanted to keep them looking nice.

Our communication with others had gotten much better. Though at times we were still very shy, our confidence increased a little more each time we received an approving nod or smile from one of the staff members.

It was on a cool day in the spring, a couple of months after our parents' visit, that Reverend Videen awoke us a little earlier than normal. We dressed quickly, anticipating the outing that we were about to go on. He'd said that we were going on a "vacation." The other kids were still sleeping, so we felt privileged to be going somewhere all by ourselves.

I watched as he quickly took our clothes from the drawer and placed them into a large, black nylon bag. When I realized that he was taking all of them, I stopped dressing and sat down on the bed.

"Let's go, Ronnie," Reverend Videen whispered.

I shook my head; Vic stopped tying his shoes and looked at me. When I pointed toward the bag that held our clothing, he dropped his laces and shrugged.

"What's the matter?" he asked.

"He's taking them all," I whispered. "All of our clothes are in there." My nervousness piqued, I felt a familiar sensation and rushed to the bathroom.

When I returned, Reverend Videen was waiting, but my brother was gone. So was the black bag.

"He's in the car already," he said, reading my thoughts. "C'mon, everything's going to be fine."

He smiled warmly and held out his hand. I took it reluctantly, and after looking around the room one last time, I followed him out to the car.

The sky was gray when we stepped outside. The sun was beginning to peek up, and the air was cool. There was a car waiting at the end of the walkway. When Mrs. Booth stepped out, I began to cry. Reverend Videen wasn't going with us, and that scared me. It was as if someone was trying to take away my security blanket.

Vic had already gotten into the car, but when he saw how upset I was, he jumped out and started to cry too. The reverend hugged us both tightly and told us to be good. He wiped our faces with his handkerchief and helped us into the car. I watched sadly from the window as we drove away. He waved to us. I waved until he disappeared from sight.

Mrs. Booth was a little different on this ride. She talked to us about the things that we'd done at the home. We warmed up to her as we began to describe the friends we'd made and the things we'd learned. She listened and laughed at some of the funny stories we told. I started to feel a little more at ease.

We rode for quite some time. Just as my eyes started to droop, we stopped and had breakfast. She treated us to pancakes and bacon at a diner near the road. I piled syrup on my pancakes until there was a small lake on my plate. It tasted so good!

When we got back on the road, I fell asleep immediately and didn't wake up until I heard a car door close. I sat up and rubbed my eyes. I nudged Vic. A small, cottage-like house stood in front of us. Mrs. Booth came around to the back door and motioned for us to get out. She grabbed our bag and lugged it to the front door.

The ringing doorbell was answered by a thin woman in a blue dress with tiny yellow flowers. There was a white apron tied around her waist, and her hair was tied up in a messy bun. She smiled at us and held the door open. Her name was Mrs. Sanderson. She led us into a small living room with shabby brown furniture. We sat down on the sofa and looked around nervously. After instructing us to behave ourselves, Mrs. Booth went into the kitchen and spoke privately to Mrs. Sanderson. We would not see Mrs. Booth again or until several years later.

As soon as they left the room, Vic and I wandered around. There was a bookcase in one corner and a scratched wooden table with dingy lace doilies on it.

A dusty phonograph caught our attention, and we both rushed over to it. Our curious fingers touched the smooth, black vinyl record that rested on it. We were both so engrossed in trying to figure out how this new thing worked that we didn't hear Mrs. Sanderson come up behind us.

"Don't touch that!" We jumped, startled by her voice. Our faces became long and nervous, like we'd been caught with our hands in the cookie jar. I cringed slightly, waiting for her to unleash an angry tirade on us, but she didn't. Instead, she wagged a warning finger at us and told us not to touch anything without asking first.

Then she turned on the phonograph while we watched with interest. She placed the needle on the spinning record. When music began to flow through the speakers, Vic and I looked at each other with surprise. This thing was very different from the radio that we'd seen at the home.

Mr. Sanderson came home while we were listening to music. He was a smallish man, with thick glasses and a bushy mustache. He reached out his hand to us. I stared at him, wondering what he wanted.

"When you meet someone," he said patiently, "you shake their hand, like this." He took Vic's hand, placed it in his own, and gave it an exaggerated shake. He turned to me next. I placed my hand in his and copied what I'd seen Vic do.

"My name is Otto. You've already met my wife, Mary. You can call us Otto and Mary, or you may call us Mother and Father. You may not call us by our first names only. Do you understand?" We nodded vigorously.

They showed us around the house, ending in a small room toward the back. There were two twin beds, one on each side of the room. They were covered with racing car bedspreads. We ran eagerly to them and jumped on top.

Mrs. Sanderson watched us for a moment and then showed us a tall, dark dresser that stood in the corner. "This is where you will put your clothes."

She left us to explore our new room. It felt strange for Vic and me to be the only ones in the room. After having shared our space with so many other kids, it almost seemed lonely. I stepped inside the closet and squatted in the corner. Tears welled up in my eyes. Though I wanted us to have a place of our own, I also wanted to go back to the home.

# Chapter 5

We'd been living with the Sanderson's for a few weeks and were getting accustomed to their routine. Our mornings consisted of eating breakfast with Mary and then helping her around the house. She was very meticulous when it came to cleaning, and I often had to do things over.

One day, we were oiling the wooden tables when Vic took the oil over to the phonograph. He began to wipe the wooden case. He poured more oil onto the rag, and some of it spilled onto the record inside. He became nervous and tried to wipe it up quickly, but when he saw how shiny the record became from the oil, he poured on more oil and wiped it. I went over and watched. The record looked really clean to me, so I picked up the others that were stacked neatly on the floor. I poured on oil, just as I had seen my brother do, and began to wipe also. Pretty soon, we'd done every record in the stack and were feeling pretty proud of ourselves.

Mary came in while we were sitting on the floor admiring our work. "What have you done?" she scolded, picking up one slick vinyl record after another.

My smile faded. Her voice had taken on that shrill pitch that had become too familiar. She was angry with us again. I felt it was only a matter of time before she would call Mrs. Booth to come and take us away.

"Go to your room," she ordered.

We slunk away to the solitude of our bedroom. Neither of us spoke. We could hear her hurrying around the room, muttering to herself. I curled up inside the closet. It had only been a week since I had stopped sleeping there to feel safe. Now with Mary being upset with us, I didn't want to be seen. Vic cried openly as he lay across his bed. I listened from inside the closet and cried too.

Sometime after noon, Mary awakened us for lunch. Vic and I were eager to get something in our stomachs and hoped that her anger with us had subsided. After washing our hands, we clamored to the table expectantly; in the middle of the table were a few crackers and some cheese on a plate. The plastic cups we normally used were halfway filled with water instead of milk or juice. Mary was in her bedroom. We looked around the empty kitchen. There were no other plates lying on the counter. After a few moments of waiting, we realized that this was to be our lunch.

It only took minutes to devour the plate of scant snacks. The water in our cups wasn't nearly enough to wash away the dryness from the saltines and thick cheese, but Mary never came into the kitchen. I guessed we weren't supposed to ask for more.

Carefully, we placed our dishes in the sink. I looked at Vic and then toward the door that led to the hallway. When he headed in that direction, I followed. Mary had not released us from our punishment. Sadly, we trudged back to our room.

I retreated to the closet and played with the small green army men that we'd been given a few weeks before. After a while, Vic came and joined me.

Hours passed, and daylight disappeared from our room. Mary had not so much as looked in on us, though we'd caught glimpses of her as she passed our door several times. Eventually, we fell asleep again. There was nothing else to do.

It was well into the evening when I felt Otto's strong arms carrying me. He placed me on my bed and covered me up. He leaned over and tousled my hair affectionately. I pretended to still be asleep until I heard him leave the room. I opened my eyes and looked into the shadows. I could hear Vic's even breathing as he slept in the other bed.

I climbed out of bed and stood beside him, hoping he would wake up. I was hungry. Neither of our parents had bothered to wake us for dinner. When he didn't wake up, I shook him. He whined and turned over, ignoring me.

I looked back at my bed. My stomach growled loudly. I couldn't wait until morning. Silently, I crept to the kitchen. The refrigerator loomed large before me. I had never been able to open it by myself before. It was too high. I jumped and reached for the handle, hung on, and pulled hard. It didn't open, so I tried again. This time the door swung open so hard that it hit the cabinet, and I fell down.

I looked inside for something to eat. There was a plate of fried chicken covered with plastic wrap on the top shelf. My stomach grumbled with anticipation. I stepped on the bottom shelf of the refrigerator and grabbed the plate.

Suddenly, my foot slipped. I fell backward into a chair, knocking it over. The plate flew out of my hands and hit the floor with a loud crash, breaking into several pieces.

Lights came on in the hallway, and Otto and Mary came rushing into the kitchen. When they turned on the light and saw the mess on the floor, they frowned disapprovingly. "What are you doing in here?" asked Mary. Her voice was sharp, and I began to cry. She came over, reached down, and stood me up. "Look at this mess!" she sputtered.

"I was hungry," I stammered through my tears.

"We do not sneak around in this house, mister! You missed dinner because you and your brother did not know how to behave. Now, clean this mess up right now! I don't work all day cleaning this house for you to mess it up whenever you want."

She crossed her arms and stood glaring at me. I looked pleadingly in Otto's direction, hoping he would convince her to be sympathetic, but he said nothing. He looked at me blankly before turning and heading back to his bedroom.

I squatted down and began to pick up the scattered food. When I looked up again, Vic had padded into the kitchen and was reaching behind the refrigerator to get the broom from the corner. He swept up the broken dish. As I held the dustpan, my stomach groaned loudly. Vic stopped and looked at me for a moment and then continued sweeping, ignoring the sounds of my hunger pangs.

We finished a few minutes later, and Mary came to make sure that the kitchen was immaculate again. Each of the chairs at the table was pushed in, and the place settings were spaced evenly. The towels were folded neatly on the counter. Everything was in its place, and the floor was swept clean. When she was satisfied that there was nothing left to do, Mary turned off the light and led us back to our beds. I got under my covers and lay there, sad, alone, and hungry.

When the morning came, I ate everything I could get my hands on. I had been messing up so much that I worried that things were about to go back to the way they had been before. Part of me was looking for the black sedan to pull into the driveway to take us back to Covenant Home.

Vic looked at me curiously as I gulped down my milk. Silently, he handed me a piece of his bacon, and I munched it down quickly.

"Stop eating like a little pig, Ronald!" Again, Mary's stern gaze was directed at me. It stopped me from eating. Victor looked from me to her and frowned. Without a word, he jumped up from the table without clearing his mess and ran out the back door.

"Get back in here!" yelled Mary.

My eyes were wide with amazement. I waited for Vic to come back, but he didn't. I didn't know what to think. He had never acted like that before. It wasn't like him to defy an adult. I put my dishes in the sink and wiped my place before running out the door behind him. I found him sitting outside under a tree, pulling at the grass. He had a scowl on his face. "What's the matter?" I asked, plopping down next to him.

"Don't like it here. She's mean to you," he answered without looking up. "I want to go home."

"You mean back to the home?"

"Nope, I mean back to *our* home, back with our own mom and dad."

I didn't say anything. I had long before stopped thinking about going back to our parents. It surprised me to hear that Vic still thought of it. Our situation with our parents had been far worse than it had been at Covenant or even with the Sandersons. "Why?" I asked quietly.

"She's mean," he hissed. "I don't like her." I nodded silently. He was right. She was mean, and I didn't like her either. Mary was furious with us when we finally went back in the house. She threatened to send us to bed again without supper. This time Otto stopped her, but by the time we sat down at the table, my appetite had disappeared. I excused myself, went to my room, got down on the closet floor, and went to sleep. Sometime later, Vic curled up beside me, and we slept there till morning.

# Chapter 6

Things continued to go downhill at the Sanderson's.

We spent more and more time in our room, punished for doing things wrong. We were never sure if we did anything right.

Mary yelled almost every day, and it made us both nervous. As a result, Vic had occasionally begun to wet himself, which only made Mary yell more. Finally, one day, the yelling stopped, but it wasn't for the best.

We'd been invited to dinner as a family over at the house of some friends of the Sanderson's. It was one of those very rare occasions where we were able to get out of the house on a social outing. As we got closer to Mr. and Mrs. Fred's house, Mary repeated the instructions that she'd given us earlier.

"You will not touch anything! You will not speak unless spoken to! You will keep quiet! And you will eat everything on your plate. Do you understand?"

We nodded, but since she was in the front seat, she didn't see us. She whirled around, leaned into the back seat, and got in our faces. "Did you hear me?"

Our heads bobbled vigorously up and down. It seemed that both of our tiny voices were lost somewhere deep in our throats. Luckily for us, we'd arrived in the driveway.

Mary turned back to the front and composed herself. By the time Mrs. Fried came out to greet us, Mary had transformed into a soft-spoken, smiling woman that we had never known existed.

"Well, aren't you two handsome little boys?" Mrs. Fried bent over in front of us and smiled.

She was an older woman. Her eyes wrinkled up when she laughed, and her hair was almost silver. Though she seemed nice, neither of us said a word. We simply stood there looking at her through bug eyes until Mary pinched us.

"Say thank you," she said through clenched teeth.

We both mumbled thank-you.

Mrs. Fried laughed and then led us all into the house.

As soon as we entered, the aroma of something delicious tempted our noses. Our house had never smelled this good. My stomach growled loudly, for which I received another pinch from Mary.

"At least I know somebody's hungry!"

Mary laughed politely at Mrs. Fred's joke, but her expression told me that she wasn't pleased.

When we walked into the living room, Mr. Fried was sitting in a big, brown chair watching television. He jumped up when he saw us and shook Otto's hand.

Mr. Fried was a very short and round man. He was bald with a graying beard. He wore suspenders and a pair of gray trousers. He sort of reminded me of the pictures we'd seen of Santa Claus.

"Please, have a seat," he said, pointing to a blue sofa covered with plastic.

Mary and Otto sat down, but when Vic and I tried to climb onto the sofa as well, Mary frowned at us sternly.

"You two sit down there!" She pointed to a space on the floor at the corner of the sofa.

Without a word, we did what we were told. We watched the television while the adults talked.

The smells from the kitchen were dizzying. We hadn't eaten since breakfast, which I couldn't understand. We hadn't done anything wrong that day, yet Mary still hadn't fixed us any lunch. Again, my stomach groaned loudly. I stole a sideways glance in the direction of the grown-ups, expecting to see Mary glaring at me, but luckily she hadn't heard me that time.

After what seemed like forever, dinner was finally ready. It was all we could do to keep from bolting to the bathroom to wash our hands, but we knew behavior like that would elicit a sharp scolding. Somehow, we managed to make our way calmly to the table, and when we did, my eyes widened with surprise. The table was covered with food, and it wasn't even a holiday.

Luckily for us, Mrs. Fried served us our plates, and she heaped them both with food. I had been worried that Mary would only give us a little and we'd be unable to ask for more.

The food was delicious. There was pot roast and chicken! Potatoes, dressing, gravy, corn, and other vegetables accompanied the meal, as well as homemade rolls. For dessert, there was chocolate cake. Everything was wonderful! I wasn't sure about Vic, but I was ready to stay there forever.

Dinner went well, and we were quite proud of the fact that we hadn't received one reprimand. But then it happened. Vic finished eating before I did. Before he got up from the table, he made sure to excuse himself. Then he pushed his chair from the table and carefully reached for his plate. But his shoes were untied. After two steps, he tripped and went sprawling to the floor. The plate crashed down with him. I gasped. It reminded me of the plate I had broken weeks earlier.

Vic jumped up quickly. He was breathing heavily, and his eyes were wide with fear. So were mine. Mama got up quickly from the table and stood in front of him.

"It's okay," said Mrs. Fried from behind them. "It was only an accident."

Mary's eyes narrowed as she stared down at Vic, her back still toward our hosts. I held my breath, wondering what she would do. The waiting was unnerving—so much so that Vic wet himself, standing right there in front of her. My mouth dropped open. It had been a while since he'd last done that. I was sure that Vic was going to get it, even in front of company.

But Mary surprised us both. Instead of yelling, she turned, gave a weak smile, and politely asked Mrs. Fried for a broom. Next, she cleaned up the broken dish. Vic and I tried to help, but she brushed us off, saying, "Nonsense, boys. It was only an accident."

To say that we were shocked would be an understatement. Neither of us knew what to do. I looked over at Otto, but he didn't say a word. Mary cleaned the entire mess by herself.

We gathered our coats once Mary finished helping Mrs. Fried with the kitchen. She apologized for not being able to stay and visit, but since she didn't have an extra set of clothes, she didn't want to be rude and have Vic there in wet clothes. Both of us were sure that we were in for something once we got in the car.

Again, nothing happened. We climbed in and waited with bated breath, but Mary still didn't say a word. Before long, the sleep monster fell upon us, and since it seemed that we had nothing to worry about, we slept soundly all the way home.

Otto carried us into the house and placed us into bed. I yawned sleepily and turned over after he pulled my shoes off and covered me up. I heard him creak down the hallway and then the soft click of the bedroom door closing. I smiled. It had been a good day.

Just as I was drifting off again, I heard the door swing back open, and Mary's swift steps filled the quiet. I didn't have to turn around to know that she was coming to our room. There was something about the way she moved that meant trouble.

"Get up!" she yelled as she flipped on the light in our room.

My body tensed as I turned around to see her scowling expression. But it wasn't directed at me. She descended on my brother like a hawk and yanked back the covers. Vic awoke with a start, his eyes wide with fear.

"I said get up!" She snatched his arm and dragged him to the floor. I watched with amazement as she continued to pull him by the arm down the hallway. I could hear Vic's screams and Mary's screams, and they kept me frozen in one place. I waited for the inevitable sound of a smack to his bottom. But when it didn't come, I inched to the doorway and peered down the hall. "This is where you use the bathroom!" Mary screamed, pointing to the toilet. "You do not embarrass me in front of other people by exercising absolutely no discipline! People will think I haven't taught you a thing!"

I had never seen her quite as angry as she was at that moment. She had Vic by the collar of his pajamas, and she was shaking him violently. Vic was in such shock that he'd grown absolutely quiet. This infuriated her.

"Do you hear me talking to you?"

Then, to my shock, I watched as she dunked my brother's head into the toilet. The water splashed. His body wiggled and his arms flailed, looking for something to hold on to. She lifted him up to more of her screams.

"l asked you a question, boy!"

Vic's coughing was uncontrollable. He couldn't get a word out if he tried. This was unacceptable to Mary. Again she submerged him, and it was then that my own scream came to life. "Stop it! Papa, help!" I ran to their bedroom and pounded furiously on the door. Where was he?

After what seemed like forever, Otto emerged, sleepily rubbing his eyes. His hair was disheveled. How could he have been sleeping through this? "Ronnie? What in the world?" he asked. My stuttered response stopped Otto short, and he strode quickly past me to the bathroom. I followed close behind. The sight of my brother made me gasp. His hair was sopping wet, and he was crying hysterically and coughing all at once. Mary still had him by the collar. "Mary" Otto yelled.

Mary whirled around in Papa's direction. Her mean glare made me shrink further behind him.

"Let the boy go!" His voice was firm and commanding. I stared up at him. I had never heard him raise his voice at her.

Mary reluctantly let go of Vic's collar, and he slumped to the floor. She gave him one last glaring look and pushed past Otto and me to her bedroom. The door slammed forcefully.

He rushed over to Vic.

"C'mon, Vic. Get up." He lifted Vic in his arms and carried him to our bedroom. "Ronnie, go get me a towel."

I raced to the linen closet, grabbed a large towel, and raced back. Vic's teeth were chattering, and his eyes were still wide with fear. Otto wiped his head dry as he peeled the pajama top off of him.

"Ronnie, get Vic some dry pajamas." I hurried over to the dresser that we shared and got out some dry pajamas. I watched as Otto dressed him. Vic's teeth were still chattering as Otto tucked him under the covers, and I was still stuck in my spot, watching it all.

"Okay, Ronnie, get into bed now. Both of you get some sleep." Reluctantly, I crawled back into my bed and pulled up the covers. When I got settled, Otto turned out the light and walked out. I listened as the bedroom door opened and softly closed.

Was that it? Didn't Otto care? He hadn't hugged us or reassured us that everything would be okay. And now we were supposed to go to sleep? I didn't understand. To say that I was afraid would be an understatement. Vic was equally as scared. I could tell from the sniffles coming from his side of the room.

"Want to sleep with me?" I whispered into the darkness.

"Yes," he whispered back. His voice was husky, still clogged with water.

He came over to my bed, and we fell back into silence, but I am sure neither of us fell asleep.

Fearfully, we stepped into the kitchen the next morning but found it empty. Our breakfast was on the table, and it was a feast. There were pancakes, eggs, and bacon, with orange juice to drink. Otto's truck was gone, and the door to the bedroom was closed. We figured Mary was locked inside; we sat down to eat hurriedly, taking nervous glances over our shoulder, expecting Mary to descend upon us at any moment. But she never arrived.

We cleared our places and cleaned up as best we could. After doing our chores, Mary still had not come out of her room, so we went outside. Vic was extremely quiet. He sat on a rock in the middle of the dusty driveway and stared at the ground. He didn't want to play any games, and while I understood, it was boring with him being so solemn.

Lunchtime came and we still had not seen Mary. Again, our food was waiting on the table, and it was in abundance. We ate quickly and disappeared into our room until Otto came home. We heard Mary finally come out, but she walked directly past our room and didn't even look in. My heart quickened and then slowed back to its normal pace.

The smells of dinner rumbled my stomach, but we were both hesitant about coming out of our room. Otto finally called us to the table, and we trudged slowly into the kitchen. When we reached our places, he said the blessing and we began to eat. Vic and I looked at each other curiously over Mary's absence from the table, again. We all ate in silence.

For almost a week, Mary stayed out of sight. We began to relax some, though getting to sleep at night was still difficult. When we did finally see her again, nothing was said about the bathroom incident. Mary even seemed to be a little nicer toward us. Maybe things would get better after all. I doubted it, but I hoped for the best.

A few weeks later, things seemed like they might turn around. I was playing in the driveway when Otto came home. "Hey, Ronnie, go get Vic. I've got a surprise for you."

I looked up from the rock castle I was building.

"Go on," he urged.

I jumped up and ran to the back door. "Vic! Come here!" I yelled through the screen door. He came to the door after a few minutes.

"What?" he asked. He'd been inside watching cartoons and didn't want to come outside.

Otto came to the porch and said, "C'mon out, Vic. I want to show you boys something."

We followed Otto back down the driveway to his truck. The first glint of red metal made us squeal with excitement. I hopped around anxiously. When he finally lifted the red tricycle and wagon from the truck, I felt breathless. Neither Vic nor I had ever received such a gift. Though there'd been plenty of bikes to ride at the home, this was something quite different. These were ours. We had no one else to share with. There were only the two of us.

Mary stood in the doorway and watched with mild amusement as we took turns riding back and forth across the pavement and into the gravel. We were a cloud of dust by the time we clambered into the house hours later. For the first time I could remember, it was dinnertime but we weren't hungry. It was also the first time in weeks that we had been happy enough to not think about leaving.

Unfortunately, the feeling was short-lived. I awoke early one morning with the hopes of getting on the tricycle first. Since I was so small, I had a hard time pedaling hard enough to pull the wagon. Because of that, Vic rarely let me ride. I figured if I got outside before him, I could practice riding. Silently, I got dressed and crept into the kitchen. There was a lingering smell of Otto's coffee in the air. He'd left for work long before the sun came up. I pushed the latch on the screen door and then went over to the corner of the washroom where the bike was standing. The wheels creaked softly as they rolled across the linoleum floor. I stopped right in front of the door and reached for the handle. I opened the door as far as I could and grabbed the handlebars. The door came swinging closed quickly and caught the bike at the pedals. It had not occurred to me that each time Vic and I rode the bike; one of us had held the door open while the other pushed everything onto the porch. Trying to do it alone was a struggle, but I didn't want to wake him. If I did, I wouldn't get a chance to ride. I pushed the handlebars, but the bike was stuck. The pedal had lodged into the netting of the screen. The creaking of the floorboards in the hallway caught my attention. Someone was awake, probably Mary. I had to hurry and get outside. If I didn't, I would get stuck doing chores. I tugged again at the bike, hard. The grating sound of the screen ripping was muted by my elation over the success of getting outside. The bike barreled onto the porch, and I hurriedly rolled it down the stairs and onto the driveway.

I had been riding for quite some time before Vic got up. He raced outside to find me covered in dust. I had fallen over quite a few times but had managed to master cycling well enough for us to take turns pulling each other in the wagon.

By the time Mary's voice carried across the yard to call us inside, it was late in the morning. Her tone seemed especially cross, but neither of us attributed it to anything other than the fact that we'd snuck outside without doing our work.

Dirty and happy, we trudged up the driveway to the porch where she was waiting. The frown on her face and the gaping hole in the screen door stopped us in our tracks. My mouth dropped open.

"Look at what you've done!"

"Didn't do that," muttered Vic.

"Of course you did that!" Mary yelled. "Get inside this house right now, and go to your room!"

"No!" Vic screamed.

I turned and stared at him. He stood there with his arms folded. His reaction surprised me, but when Mary grabbed him by the arm and yanked him, I began to scream too.

"I-I-I did it," I stuttered. "It was an accident!"

My admission didn't matter. She had already decided that she was angry with both of us. Vic kicked and screamed all the way to the bedroom and continued long after she left us there. We soon tired and fell asleep.

Sometime later, we were awakened by a vigorous shake. I raised my tear-stained face from the pillow and looked up to see

Mrs. Booth standing over us. She was holding our jackets. I looked around and saw two black bags sitting on the floor by the door. What we'd wanted—yet feared—was happening. We were leaving. The Sanderson's could no longer deal with us.

Red Cross report dated March 31, 1951:

> Worker feels this placement to be unsatisfactory. The children act out their hostilities frequently, Victor more than Ronnie. Mrs. Sanderson is compulsive in her drive to control the children. Although warm, she is not understanding of the children's behavior and has little patience with them. She expects conformity to all her wishes; therefore, the children are a disappointment to her. At present she is willing to have the children leave for a new placement. During earlier visits, Mrs. Sanderson could not permit herself this action as she has some guilt about her deficiencies. Today, she blames the children for all troubles. Both children have reacted by being subtly destructive. They have marked walls and torn sheets. Victor will dawdle on his way to and from school. Mrs. Sanderson has been specific in setting a time limit for his return, but Victor but is often late. Ronnie is more passive in his behavior and will make pitiful attempts to please his foster parents. The children will be removed from this home as soon as a suitable home can be found.

> The parents have indicated their wish to have the children returned to them as soon as this possibility has been fully explored. A decision will be made as to whether it is feasible for the children to be returned. Both children have expressed their wish to be with their father and mother. Although the parents seem lacking in their ability to accept complete responsibility for these children, both Victor and Ronnie need the security of warm emotional acceptance.

# Chapter 7

My feelings were mixed as we rode away from the Sanderson. I was happy that we were leaving. Living there had been more horrible than it had been fun. Mary's unpredictable mood swings and constant chastisement made it hard for my brother and me to relax.

But I was also sad. Even though I liked the kids and the workers at the home, I wondered how long it would be before we'd get another chance at having a family. I drifted off to sleep. In my dreams, I imagined what the perfect parents would be like. I awoke with a smile on my face to the feel of soft hands tugging at my arm. When I opened my eyes, my smile faded. Mama? Where were we?

I sat up quickly and looked around in shock. The faces of my mother and father beamed down at me. I looked over at Vic. We were back with our parents!

I climbed out of the car, my insides bubbling with uncertainty. I didn't know whether to be happy or sad. My father grabbed our bags from the car, while Mama took us each by the hand.

I looked back at Mrs. Booth. She stood by the car door and waved at us. I waved back sadly. I wasn't sure I wanted to be there. I turned back around and looked at the house that stood in front of us. It was small, old, and weather-beaten. The wooden shingles hung loosely from the roof, threatening to fall off at any moment. When we reached the porch, we stepped carefully over the holes in the steps.

The inside did not look much better. The hardwood floor was dull and dusty. There was a small wooden table in the corner, with three wooden chairs. A fourth one stood off to the side, leaning against the wall due to a broken leg.

There was a shabby brown sofa next to a matching chair that sat in front of a desolate-looking fireplace. It was freezing outside and equally as cold inside.

"Welcome home, boys." Mama's voice was tentative; as if she wasn't really sure she meant what she'd just said.

I looked over at Vic. He was taking in our new surroundings too. My father walked into another room with our bags. "Boys," he called gruffly. We followed him into a tiny room.

There was a bookshelf in one corner, a dresser in another, and not much more. "This is where you'll be sleeping." Vic and I looked at him. There were no beds! Instead, there was a pile of blankets on the floor off to the side of the bookcase.

Our father motioned toward them as if reading our minds. He said, "You will spread those out and sleep on them. We'll get you something better a little later, when I can get some more work." The emotionless tone of his voice chilled me, more than the iciness of the air around me.

"Me and your mama are going to get your brothers. You two unpack these bags and put your clothes away. We'll be back shortly. You understand?"

We both bobbed our heads. Brothers! We didn't know we had more than one. Did they mean Ralph Jr.? I was almost afraid to ask, but it didn't matter. Vic beat me to it. "Do you mean little Ralph, sir?"

"Yeah," he answered shortly. Without another word, he disappeared. We heard the front door open and shut and then the sputtering of the old Buick that had been parked in the driveway.

Neither of us said a word as we unpacked our belongings, doing our best to try and shove everything into the limited drawer space. Finally, we realized that it was impossible to get it all in, and we left some of our clothes in the bags.

"I'm hungry." My stomach had started growling on the long ride here since we hadn't been able to eat before leaving the Sanderson's. fact is, they had barely looked at us as Mrs. Booth hustled us out the front door. It was almost as if they pretended not to know us. I thought about Vic's wish from not so long before, to return to our mother and father. I wondered if he was happy, so I asked, "Are you glad we're back?"

Vic shrugged. "Don't know yet. Let's find something to eat."

We went back into the kitchen and looked around. The narrow refrigerator that stood in the corner was white. Vic went to it quickly and opened the door. Emptiness stared back at us. My stomach groaned anxiously. There was a bottle of milk in the door, a few brown eggs, a stick of butter. Vic's face fell, full of disappointment. There was nothing for us to do but sit and wait. Darkness fell, and with it the room got colder. The house creaked with the blowing wind, and Vic and I huddled on the floor of our room, grabbing the blankets to keep warm. It had been over two hours since our parents had left. Along with the hunger in my stomach, there sat a sinking feeling of being abandoned.

I was dozing off when I heard the rickety sound of the Buick's engine making its way into the driveway. The snap of the car doors jolted Vic awake, but neither of us moved. The front door opened and closed, and immediately the sound of a baby's cry filled the house. We jumped up and ran into the other room to see our little brother but stopped short. There were two babies!

Wide eyed, I looked from one to the other. It wasn't hard to tell which one was Ralph, but who was this other baby?

"This is your brother, Simon," Mama said as she moved toward us. I looked at him. He was tiny, bundled up in several blankets. He reminded me of the way Ralph had looked the day that we'd been taken away over a year ago.

"Hello, Simon," Vic said solemnly as he looked down on our new brother. Then he turned cheerfully to Ralph. Ralph was a toddler and wobbly on his legs. He stood near Mama. When Vic spoke to him, he looked in our direction. He looked from Vic to me and began to cry. He didn't recognize us. He turned back to Mama and clutched her leg. She picked him up and cooed at him, rocking him into silence. For a moment, I wished I were him.

Dinner was a scant helping of beans and a glass of milk. I received a stern glare when I asked for seconds and realized quickly that there wasn't any more to be had. My stomach groaned its protest in the middle of the night as Vic and I lay in our blankets on the floor. Sleep was a long time coming.

It didn't take long for Ralph to get to know us. After a few days, he wobbled to us whenever he saw us. Though we were delighted by this recognition, with it came the responsibility of watching his every move.

Every morning started out the same. My father left well before the sun came up, before any of us were awake. Vic and I awakened to the sounds of Simon's cries. Mama hustled around fixing his bottle and getting him dressed. We scurried around fetching diapers and other things that she asked us for. She fixed a quick breakfast, usually consisting of toast and cheese with a glass of milk. It was never enough, but we were not permitted to say so.

A couple of weeks after our arrival, my parents decided that they could not afford to leave Ralph at the sitter any longer. That was when Mama began leaving him at home with us. "Keep an eye on your brother," she would say as she left with Simon in her arms. Vic and I were only 4 and 5 years old at this time.

It was hard to amuse Ralph. We didn't have many things to play with except the small army men that we'd brought with us, but Mama had already told us that we could not let Ralph play with them because he could swallow them, so we were forced to find other ways to keep him from crying.

One evening while we were waiting for Mama to come home, Ralph would not be quiet. It was later than usual, and he had already drunk all of his bottles. The house was cold, and we sat shivering. "Let's make a fire," said Vic. I stared at him.

What can we use?" I asked. We'd barely seen our father make a fire, let alone ever made one ourselves. Daddy had always told us that we were too little to make the fire, though we weren't too little to carry the heavy bundles of wood. Ralph was still wailing, and I wondered what good making a fire would do in making him get quiet.

"Quiet, Ralph. Don't cry," I said pleadingly.

I watched as Vic walked over to the fireplace and picked up a piece of kindling from the stack of wood. When he found a piece that he liked, he took it over to the stove. Next, he turned the knob on the stove. The hissing sound of the gas filled the air.

I looked at him with surprise. "Vic! You're not supposed to do that! We're going to get in trouble!"

"It's cold," he said. "We have to stop Ralph from being cold." He found the matches and struck one. Nothing happened. The pungent smell of gas continued to fill the room. Vic tried again, and again nothing happened.

"Turn it off, Vic," I whined.

"Don't you start crying too," he said. I sniffed loudly and poked out my lip, angry that he had implied that I was going to be a crybaby like our little brother.

Vic struck the match again, and it sparked. The fire spread as he put the match to the burner like we'd seen Mama do many times. I watched in awe, scarcely aware of the fact that Ralph had become quiet at the sight of the glowing fire. It wasn't until he squealed with delight that I paid attention to him again. Both of us were watching Vic. Just as he stuck the kindling in the fire, Mama walked in. "What is going on in here?" Her voice startled us all. I jumped, Ralph began to wail, and Vic dropped the kindling on the floor. The fire quickly consumed the small piece of wood and searched for something to keep it alive. It found a nearby rug and began to blaze.

Mama dropped the bag in her arm, set Simon down, and rushed over to the growing fire. She jumped up and began to stomp furiously on the rug, trying to squelch the fire. All of us stood still and watched her with our mouths open. We didn't hear our father come in. Without a word, he rushed over and began stomping on the fire alongside Mama. Finally, they were able to put it out. Ashes covered the area, and a cloud of smoke floated around the room. There was a black scorch mark on the floor.

Simon started crying, and Ralph began coughing from the smoke. Mama ran to attend to them, and our father turned on us. His eyes held a fire of their own. "Thought I told you boys not to mess with fire," he said.

"B-b-but it was cold, sir," Vic replied, trembling slightly.

"You disobeyed me, boy. Ronnie, go run get a switch," he ordered. I was stuck in my place. Though both of our parents had threatened to whip us several times since our arrival, they had, until that point, not laid a hand on us. I didn't even know what a switch was! "I said move, boy!" I began to cry but still didn't move. I couldn't. I didn't know what to do. Taking my inaction as disobedience, my father stormed past us and out the front door. He grabbed a small branch from the tree in front of our house and returned to the house. Vic's eyes widened as Daddy came toward him holding the switch. *Swat!* Vic howled with pain as Daddy smacked him on the backside with the switch several times. "Don't ever disobey me again!" A swat followed each syllable of his sentence. He let go of Vic's arm and moved toward me. I moved backward in fear, but he reached out and pulled me to him. "And you," he said to me, breathing heavily, "when I tell you to do something, you do it!" He swatted me three quick times and let go. We were sent to our room, our behinds stinging and our pride hurt. We lay down on our blankets sniffling, eventually drifting off to sleep.

During the weeks that followed that incident, it seemed that Vic and I were the only ones getting thinner. Both Simon and Ralph always had enough to eat. Mama often commented that people donated the formula for the babies. I wished we were so lucky. The nights were that much longer with nothing in our stomachs. The cheese sandwiches that were left for our lunches did not calm the growing pangs of hunger in our stomachs. Each night, I wished that Mrs. Booth would come back and take us. It didn't matter where we went, as long as we left that place.

# Chapter 8

Christmas was coming around again, but there were none of the festivities that we'd experienced at Covenant. The weather turned bitingly cold, and we spent most days huddled under our blankets with Ralph, waiting for our parents to come home and start a fire.

About a week before Christmas, we woke up late. The house was unusually quiet. I got up and scurried across the cold floor to the kitchen. No one was there, and things seemed different. The familiar smell of my father's coffee did not fill the room. I raced to the window and looked outside. Our old Buick was still parked in the driveway, which meant that our father was still home.

I went back to the room and burrowed under the covers. I decided to wait there until Mama made us get up. If my father was still home, maybe we would all be home together. I must have drifted back off to sleep because Mama rushed into our room and woke us. Her face was stained with tears, but she appeared to be angry with us. "Get up and watch your brother!" she growled at us as she plunked Ralph down on my legs. She disappeared quickly, and I listened as she moved around in the kitchen getting Simon ready. Her sniffles carried into our room, and I got up to see what the matter was.

"Mama?" She turned on me, and I saw the tears running down her face. I had never seen her cry before. "What's the matter, Mama? Where's Daddy?"

She dropped the baby bottle that she'd been holding, and formula splattered onto the floor. Some of the warm milk hit my bare foot, and I jumped. Mama glared at me through the tears in her eyes. "Shut your mouth!" she screamed.

Vic ran into the room, curious about the commotion. "What's wrong?" he asked. Though he was asking me, his question infuriated Mama more.

"Your father left," she spat.

"But the car . . ." I began. I was confused. Why was she mad that he left? He left every morning, didn't he?

"He left and he isn't coming back!" she yelled.

It took a moment for that to sink in. Where had he gone? Why had he left?

Vic voiced my thoughts. "Why, Mama?" His question was innocent, but the resentment in Mama's eyes flashed angrily.

Her words were equally as venomous: "He left 'cause of you two!"

She turned, picked up Simon, and walked out the door. The Buick fired up and sputtered out of the driveway. She'd left us alone, with no breakfast.

My heart sunk as I thought about my mother's words. I tried to think of what we had done that made our father leave. I concluded that it was because we were bad kids. After the spanking we had gotten because of the fire, we had received them somewhat regularly. My father was always angry with us. We waited until well after dark for our mother to come home. Ralph had long since run out of bottles, so we gave him regular milk from the refrigerator. It didn't sit well on his stomach and gave him diarrhea. The house smelled of sour diapers. When Mama came in, we cringed, expecting her to yell at any moment. Instead, she staggered past us into her bedroom and closed the door. Vic and I looked at each other. Where was Simon? When it became apparent that she wasn't coming out again, we gave Ralph another regular milk bottle and went to bed hungry.

Our days and nights continued in about that fashion for almost a week. Some days, Mama remembered to leave us something, but most times she acted as if we weren't there. She left early in the morning and came in very late at night. We hadn't seen Simon in a long time, but neither of us was willing to risk setting off Mama's temper by asking where he was.

It was no surprise when Mrs. Booth returned one morning to pick us up. There was another woman with her, and she took Ralph away in a separate car. We rode for several hours before stopping. Mrs. Booth fed us hamburgers and French fries. She even treated us to milkshakes! Vic and I savored the taste of the creamy ice cream on our tongues. We rode for a few more hours into a rural area, passing several large fields with cows, goats, and horses. Vic and I looked out the window at all the animals in amazement. We'd never seen so many of them in one place. We made a game out of trying to see who could count the most of each type of animal. We'd become so engrossed that we didn't pay attention to the fact that we were approaching a house. It wasn't until the car came to a stop that we focused on our surroundings.

The gravel driveway was long and winding and led up to a tall two-story house with gray siding. Just beyond the house was a red barn. The paint was peeling, weathered from many winter rains. On the right was a small brown shack. It was impossible to imagine anybody living in something so tiny. The land sprawled out for what seemed like forever. There was a gate to the left, where a bunch of cows were grazing. Though Mrs. Booth had told us to stay put, we jumped out of the car and ran over to the fence, peeping through the slats at them. They ignored us and continued chewing on the grass. I reached between the wires in the fence. I wanted to touch them. I had never been that close to any animal other than a dog. But they were not willing to cooperate, remaining just out of my reach. Disappointed, I moved from the fence and kicked rocks up the driveway. The squawk of some wandering chickens caught our attention. At the far end of the field was a long, narrow, white chicken house. There were bunches of chickens strutting around, stopping occasionally to scratch and peck at the ground. Vic and I ran to the other side of the gate and squatted down to watch them. We were fascinated. *Where are we?* I wondered.

The sound of a screen door banging closed, followed by women's voices, and caught my attention. I looked up the road and saw Mrs. Booth talking to a woman. Vic looked at me. We quietly crept closer to the door so that we could hear.

"Look, Mrs. Booth," the woman said. "I told the agency that we only wanted to take in girls. Boys are much too difficult to rise."

Mrs. Booth glanced around the land and said, "Mrs. Borg, surely you can understand my situation. These young boys have had a difficult time, but I can assure you that they will not be any trouble to you. They really need a home."

We held our breath and waited while Mrs. Borg stood quietly, contemplating what Mrs. Booth had just said. Silently we willed her to say yes. As far as we could tell, this place was wonderful. Besides, we worried that if she did not take us in, Mrs. Booth would be forced to take us back to our mother.

Mrs. Borg sighed loudly. "All right, they can stay. But if I have one lick of trouble from them, I am going to call you to come back for them."

"Of course," Mrs. Booth agreed. She turned in the direction of the car. "Vic, Ronnie," she called out to us. We jumped out from our hiding place and ran toward her. She frowned at our disobedience for not having stayed in the car but didn't say anything. "Boys, this is Mrs. Borg. You'll be staying here with her and her husband."

Upon getting a closer look, neither Vic nor I were sure what to make of Mrs. Borg. She was a short, portly woman wearing a yellow housedress with an apron. She stared down at us with eyes that didn't have a smile hidden anywhere in them. Nothing about her appearance welcomed us. My voice left my throat until Mrs. Booth nudged us. "Hello, ma'am," we both said shyly. She looked each of us over, drawing us to her, checking our hair, ears, and even inside our mouths, as if she were inspecting puppies. Finally, she said, "Hello." Her voice was gruff and uninviting. I began to think that staying there would not be such a wonderful idea after all. But it was settled. Mrs. Borg would take us in provided we didn't cause any trouble. As best as I could tell, we never did. But like most anything else, that was a matter of opinion. And so, for the third time in less than three years, Vic and I stood at the end of a road, waving good-bye to Mrs. Booth in her black sedan. For the third time, we had no idea what we were in for. But for the millionth time, I was scared.

# Chapter 9

If we'd been unsure of how to read Mrs. Borg upon meeting her, Mr. Borg made things crystal clear. His old, beat-up Ford came barreling down the gravel driveway, heaped with bags of sod, grain, and other items from the feed store in town.

Vic and I had been sitting on the porch. After Mrs. Booth left, we hadn't known what to do. Mrs. Borg didn't invite us into the house. She'd stood on the porch, watched the sedan disappear, looked at us with disdain, and then returned inside the house. When Mr. Borg got out of the truck, our eyes widened. He was a tall, heavyset man with thick, bushy eyebrows and what seemed to be a permanent scowl on his face. We watched as he grabbed a sack of feed from the bed of the truck and slung it over his massive shoulders. He walked over to the weather-beaten barn and disappeared inside. After several trips, he looked over at us.

"Who are you?" His gruff voice made me so nervous that I started to shake. "Well?" he boomed impatiently.

Mrs. Borg came to the screen door. "Agency brought 'these boys," she said flatly. "Told 'the agency we wanted girls, but she says these boys were all she had. She didn't have nowhere else for the boys to go."

Mr. Borg looked us over and grunted. "Well, what are your names?"

"I'm Vic," my brother answered. "This is Ronnie," he said when I didn't answer after a few seconds.

Mr. Borg looked us over again, grunted, and headed back toward the truck. He shouldered another sack of feed and then looked in our direction. "If you're going to live here, you'll have to earn your keep. When I come home with a load, you'll pitch in until we're done."

We stood up but were frozen to our spots. We weren't quite sure what he wanted us to do. When we didn't move, Mr. Borg's scowl deepened. "Get over here and grab a sack of feed—now!" The thunder in his voice loosened the glue that seemed to be on the bottoms of our feet. Vic and I scrambled over to the truck. "Hold your arms out," he said. We did as we were told. Mr. Borg dropped a sack onto our waiting arms. The heavy load staggered us, and we tumbled to the ground. I started to cry. "Quit that sissy crying!" he bellowed. He bent down and grabbed the sack. "Hold your arms out." I sniffled loudly, got to my feet, and held my arms out as I had been told. Mr. Borg dropped the sack onto us again with the same amount of force as before. We staggered and fell again but got quickly to our feet. After several more failed attempts, Mr. Borg decided to give us smaller sacks to carry. We managed to half-carry, half-drag those sacks to the barn and stack them as we were instructed. We worked for over two hours before finally trudging into the house. We were covered in dirt, and my arms and legs burned. When we got inside, Mr. Borg disappeared. Since it was our very first time inside the house, we had no idea where to go, so we stood in the middle of the front hallway and waited. The smell of fried pork chops drifted under my nose, and my stomach lurched. It had been hours since we'd eaten, but after what we had gone through with our parents, it felt more like days. Several minutes passed before Mrs. Borg stepped out of the kitchen and noticed us standing there,

"Well, for goodness sakes, get over there by the hand pump on the porch and get cleaned up!" Our legs moved heavily toward the sink on the porch. It was dark, and we had no idea how to work a hand pump. Mrs. Borg showed us how to use the pump by moving the handle up and down. Water started coming out, and we quickly washed our hand and faces. We also realized that there was no indoor plumbing.

Mr. Borg stepped out of a tiny room. His size intimidated us once more as he loomed over us, and we stood still. He frowned, stepped around us, and disappeared again onto the porch. We hurried back into the kitchen, which had the only light we saw.

The kitchen was small and dingy. An old refrigerator hissed in the corner as if it was going to conk out at any moment. The paint on the white cabinets was peeling, and the linoleum on the floor had curled up around the edges. A small table stood at the far end underneath a drawstring light.

Mrs. Borg was standing over the wood-burning stove with her fork in a pan of hot grease and her back to us. We stood there for a few moments, waiting for her to turn around. When she didn't, Vic spoke up.

"Excuse me, ma'am, what do you want us to do now?"

The sound of Vic's tiny voice startled Mrs. Borg, and she jumped in surprise. The grease crackled, and some of it popped out onto her arm. She winced in pain and then whirled around with a scowl. "Don't you ever come sneaking up on me again? Do you hear me?"

We both nodded vigorously. Vic bit his lip to keep from crying. Seeing our faces, she softened a bit and pointed toward the table. "Go on over there and sit down. Mister will be in here in a minute, and you all can eat." We scrambled over to the table and sat down. Mr. Borg came and sat down a few minutes later. Again he frowned at us but didn't say a word. Mrs. Borg brought over plates of pork chops, rice, and cabbage and sat them in front of us. When she sat down, Vic and I waited expectantly. At the Sanderson's, we'd been taught to wait until Otto began eating before we ate. Though we weren't sure if the same thing applied here, we didn't want to run the risk of being scolded again.

"Is there something wrong that you can't eat my food?" Mrs. Borg asked, staring at us. She had already begun to eat her food, but Mr. Borg sat looking at us.

"No, ma'am," we both whispered. A few more moments passed, and she looked our way again. Neither of us had moved, though both of our stomachs were rumbling ferociously.

Mrs. Borg dropped her fork against her plate, and the clanging sound made me jump. She was clearly angry with us. "Start eating now, or else I'll just take those plates from you and you can go to bed hungry for all I care!"

She continued to mutter under her breath about us being ungrateful and how she'd told those people that she didn't want boys anyhow. My heart was racing in my chest. I certainly didn't want her taking my plate, but when I stole a glance at Mr. Borg, he hadn't moved. He was still looking us over as if he was trying to figure out something about us.

"All right, that's it!"

I gasped when I saw her get up and reach for our plates. Vic's eyes widened. The idea of going to bed without eating was suddenly about to become a reality. Why did it seem that we were always being punished?

"Leave them alone, Ruth!" Mr. Borg's voice bellowed into the silence, quickening my heartbeat even more. Mrs. Borg stopped in her tracks and stared at her husband. By the expression on her face, it was obvious that she didn't take too kindly to the tone he had taken with her in front of us, but it was equally obvious that he didn't care.

"Look at me," he commanded. Both Vic and I did as we were told. I felt a chill in my body, and I trembled slightly. "You boys been taught not to touch your food 'til the man of the house eats. That right?" We nodded our heads vigorously. I felt the air sail out of my body in relief. Thank God he understood!

"What kind of nonsense . . ." Mrs. Borg began.

"Hush, Ruth," he interrupted her. "Good to know you boys been taught right," he said. His face softened some, but I wouldn't have called his expression a smile. He picked up his fork and scooped some rice into his mouth. I happily followed suit, while Vic opted to dig right into his pork chop. Mrs. Borg looked from one to the other of us before sitting back down. Not another word was said at the table, and that suited me just fine.

# Chapter 10

"Ouch!"

My startled cry caused Vic to jump straight up in bed and with good reason. When he looked over to where I was laying, he saw a huge crow pecking at my toes through the covers. My eyes widened with terror as I tried to squirm away from the flutter of its wings and the sharp peck of its beak. Where had this mad bird come from?

"Shoo!" Vic ran over and flailed his arms at the bird, hoping to make it go away. But the bird kept hovering around me, squawking every so often as if taunting me. It was obvious that the enormous bird was not intimidated by Vic's feeble shouts, so my brother picked up a shoe that was near the bed. Just as he was about to hurl it, Mrs. Borg came in.

"All right, Nicodemus let 'the boys alone."

And just like that, the bird flew away from us and landed on Mrs. Borg's shoulder. Both Vic and I stared at her, our mouths hanging wide open. "Boy, put that shoe down. Don't 'cha be throwing things at' Nicodemus. I sent him in here to wake you two lazy things up!"

The shoe dropped to the floor with a thud, but still neither of us moved or said a word. Not only was the bird Mrs. Borg's, but she'd sent it into our room to wake us up. That was definitely something new to us.

"Well, don't just stand there! Get your clothes on, and come on in here if you want to eat breakfast. You got chores to do today!" She turned, the bird still on her shoulder, and walked downstairs to the kitchen.

For about half a minute, we just stood there. I had gotten over being scared and was pretty amazed by the trained bird. I chuckled a little. The nips hadn't really hurt, but they had surely surprised the daylights out of me. I grabbed a pair of pants and a shirt from the small wooden dresser that held our clothes and dressed hurriedly.

When we reached the kitchen, Mrs. Borg had placed two steaming bowls of oatmeal on the table, along with two glasses of milk. Since ours were the only dishes on the table, we felt safe in assuming that Mr. Borg would not be sitting down with us. Mrs. Borg was nowhere in sight, but we could hear Nicodemus squawking outside on the porch, so we figured she was close by. The two of us ate quickly and quietly, making sure to clean up after ourselves once we finished. When we stepped out onto the porch, Mrs. Borg was waiting for us. "'Bout time you two got out here. C'mon now so we can get started before the mister gets upset."

She stepped down onto the soft dirt road and walked toward the barn. Out of nowhere, Nicodemus swooped down and perched on her shoulder.

"Rover, Jenny, get on over here," she called.

Neither Vic nor I had a clue who Rover or Jenny were until two dogs came bounding over from behind the house. Mrs. Borg stopped when the dogs reached her. "Sit down, you mangy things!" The two animals immediately obeyed her and looked up, awaiting the next command. She beckoned both of us over to where she was standing.

"This here's Rover," she said, pointing to the large black Newfoundland. "And this one here is Jenny." Jenny, a brown-and-white collie, wagged her tail vigorously as Mrs. Borg patted her on the head. I inched over to the dogs but stopped when Rover tensed up. "Take your time, boy. Rover doesn't take too well to folks he don't know." I stood there for a moment and decided to approach Jenny first. She seemed to be a little friendlier. I rubbed her head, and she responded by licking me playfully.

I looked behind me and saw my brother still standing in the same spot. "Come on, Vic. She's nice." I moved over so that he could stand next to me.

Mrs. Borg watched us, and so did Rover. After a while, I think he got jealous because he came over and nudged his way in between us so that he could get some of our attention. I laughed as the warmth of his tongue tickled my fingers.

"All right, that's enough," Mrs. Borg said gruffly. She turned and trudged ahead toward the barn. As if they understood her words, both Jenny and Rover tagged along behind. There was nothing left for Vic and me to do but follow as well.

It had been too dark and we'd been too nervous the night before to pay much attention to the inside of the barn. But as we stood in the middle of it in the early morning hours, we noticed the sweet smell of bales of hay that were stacked on one side. There was an old, yellow tractor parked near the window along with several tools, and in the corner were the bags of feed that we'd helped Mr. Borg carry in. There were three stalls, though no horses were inside them. Mrs. Borg paused a moment to let us look around before getting down to the business of chores.

"Grab one of them pails over there, both of you." We followed the direction of her extended finger to a corner of the barn near the door, where there were several metal pails stacked inside of one another. Vic took one and handed me another, and we rushed back to her side, awaiting her next instruction. It was kind of exciting since neither of us had ever been in a place so big, with so many animals.

"See those barrels right there?" she asked, pointing again but in a different direction. We nodded once we spotted the weathered wooden barrels that stood next to the bags of feed. "Open one of them up and scoop some of that feed in both of them pails." Vic and I looked at each other and then took off in a race to see who could get there first. He beat me by a half a second and slid the lid off of the first barrel he came to. We stood on our tiptoes and peeked inside. The barrel was half full of a mixture of corn and grain, and a large metal scoop sat on top. Since Vic got there first, he would get to be the one to scoop the feed while I held the pail. The only problem was that the barrel was tall, and the feed was low inside. He stared into the barrel and then tried to stretch his arm to reach the metal scoop. But of course, he couldn't. Vic thought for a moment. While I waited, I stole a glance over at Mrs. Borg, who was busying herself with something on a shelf behind one of the stalls. Silently, I willed Vic to hurry up with an idea. Something told me that if Mrs. Borg became impatient, it could easily erupt into anger.

"Ronnie, lay that pail down," Vic said. I looked quizzically at my brother. Lay it down? I had no idea what he was talking about. Reading the confusion in my face, he grabbed the pail from my hands and set it on the ground, upside down.

"Oh," I said, as I finally understood what he was doing. With the pail on the ground, he had a stepping stool that allowed him to reach down far enough into the barrel. Vic scooped feed into the pail he had brought. I watched as the mixture of corn slid off the scoop and into the pail with a clanging sound. It had a strong, sweet smell, and I wondered what made this corn different from the kind we ate at dinnertime. Once the pail was full, I sat it down on the ground and raced over to get another empty one. Mrs. Borg looked over at me when I breezed by, and I could feel her eyes watching me as I grabbed another pail and ran back to where Vic was. *Please don't let her get angry*, I thought as I held the pail for my brother. "Hurry up, Vic," I whispered. He was about to protest but then seemed to think better of it after looking over his shoulder and seeing that we were being watched. He shoveled faster, and when he finished I set the pale next to the first one. Vic carefully replaced the lid on the barrel while I returned the empty pail. Mrs. Borg was still looking at us, but her expression didn't appear angry. In fact, it was probably the closest thing to a smile we'd seen from her so far. We lugged the full buckets of feed over to where she was standing, but before we could put them down, she turned and walked out of the barn.

"Let's go," she called over her shoulder.

We followed her around the side of the barn over to the small brown shack we'd noticed the day before. As we got closer, I could hear faint clucking sounds growing louder. It was a henhouse. Mrs. Borg swung the door open. We were about to step inside when she stopped us. "You go in there with them full pails, and the hens are going to swarm all over you." She reached in my pail and took a fistful of feed. "Stay here. When they come out, take your hand and start scattering it on the ground out here." She disappeared and then reappeared shortly, a bunch of hens strutting out behind her. We watched as she sprinkled a bit of the corn, and the birds anxiously pecked it up as soon as it hit the ground. "Go on and get started," she said. Holding the pail by the handle and the bottom, I began shaking feed onto the ground. Vic did the same.

"Not like that!" she shouted gruffly. "Use your hand like you saw me do. And don't stand so close together. Spread out some, else you going to have a fight on your hands." I went left while Vic went right, sprinkling food out the way we'd seen Mrs. Borg do it. Before I knew it, there were hens and roosters everywhere. There were red ones, white ones, and black ones. In all, I think there must have been about fifty of them. When the pails were empty, we stood there and watched the birds scratch and peck at the ground. The roosters strutted around, not really eating as much as they were putting on a show for the hens around them. "Let's go," Mrs. Borg called. "We don't got all morning!"

Vic turned to follow her into the henhouse, but I was still stuck watching the chickens in front of me. "Ronnie let's go!" Vic shouted. He came back and tugged me by the arm into the henhouse.

Inside were several rows of nests. The floor was covered with hay, and stray feathers were scattered here and there. Mrs. Borg had already made her way to the first row of nests. She had a large basket in her hand. "Get some of that hay over there," she said, pointing to a broken-up bale of hay near the door. Vic and I did as we were told. I inhaled the sweetness of the hay as I grabbed a handful. "Put it in the bottom of your buckets like this." She held up her already lined basket to show us, and we copied what we saw. Next, she reached into one of the nests and pulled out two eggs. Both of our eyes widened to the size of saucers. We'd never seen eggs come from anywhere other than a store. "Don't just stand there." Both of us ran to a row of nests and began reaching inside. The eggs felt warm, and that too was a surprise to me. I looked across at Vic, and he seemed to be having a good time doing this new chore. We each finished our rows and moved on to the next. Fifteen minutes later, we were carrying our nearly full buckets into the house. Though they weren't very heavy, it was a chore to keep the eggs from rolling around so they wouldn't crack. Rover and Jenny's darting around and in between us made it that much more difficult. When we got to the house, Mrs. Borg told us to set them on top of the kitchen table while she went to get a bowl of water. "Ronnie, you dip 'the eggs in the water, and Vic's going to dry 'the eggs," she said, passing him a small towel. She came back with two very large, empty bowls, which she said were for the eggs once they were washed. I took an egg, carefully dipped it in the water, and then passed it to Vic. And then I did another. By about the fourth egg, Mrs. Borg bellowed at us about moving too slow. The impatience in her voice made me so nervous that the next three eggs I dipped slipped through my fingers and cracked. This, of course, only made her mad, and she fussed the whole time that she was at the sink changing the water.

# Chapter 11

Over the next few weeks, we settled into a routine on the Borg's' farm. After our first full day of chores, Mrs. Borg added several others that kept us occupied from six in the morning until well into the twilight hours. Most days, she watched us for the first couple of hours and then disappeared into the house to do her cleaning. As soon as she left us, Vic and I usually found ways to amuse ourselves in between feeding animals, collecting milk and eggs, and pulling weeds in Mrs. Borg's small garden. We spent a lot of time in the barn. In fact, it was our favorite place because there were so many places to hide. It was like our secret clubhouse, except it wasn't really a secret.

Though neither Vic nor I were fond of chores to begin with, cleaning the pigpen was probably the thing we hated the most. It seemed as though the area was always muddy, and it was often hard to tell the difference between the wet earth and the manure that we were supposed to clean up. Because of this, we were constantly cleaning our raggedy tennis shoes to rid them of the stench that lingered behind us. We were in the midst of cleaning our shoes one afternoon when Vic suddenly had to go to the bathroom. I wasn't sure what was wrong with him, but he had been having a terrible stomachache all day and had made several trips to the outhouse already. When he bolted from the bale of hay that we were sitting on and took off running, I knew where he was headed. Even though I felt bad for him, I couldn't help but chuckle. I mean, it *was* a little funny. I was still scraping my shoe with a stick when I heard my name being called from a distance. I jumped up and ran around the side of the barn toward the porch. I was almost there when I heard the muffled voice again. It was Vic calling me from the outhouse. I ran toward the sound of his voice and stopped outside the door. "I'm right here," I answered when he called me again. "What is it?"

"There's no paper in here for me to wipe," he said. "Can you go get some?" I suppressed a laugh. The idea of Vic stuck with no toilet paper was indeed funny. If I had wanted to be mean, I could have left and just let him stay in there. But I thought better of it. I knew how bad the smell could get in there, and since he'd been running in there all day, I figured he could really be sick. My leaving him stranded like that wouldn't have been nice. Besides, Vic was always really good about coming with me when I needed to go in the middle of the night.

"I'll be right back," I called to him. I dashed off to the house, flung open the screen door to the porch, and hurried to the cabinet in the hallway. I was pulling a roll of the stiff paper from its package when Mrs. Borg came up behind me.

"What are you doing in my house?" I hadn't heard her coming, and the sound of her voice suddenly told me that she was right behind me and she startled the daylights out of me. I fell over from my crouched position but jumped up quickly. She was glaring down at me, and my words got stuck in my throat as they always seemed to do when I stood before her.

"How many times I have to tell y'all to stay outta my house? You don't come in here until I call you!" Her face was reddening, an obvious sign that her anger was almost at a boil.

"Y-y-yes, ma'am, b-b-but, my b-b-brother—" I began, but she cut me off before I could finish.

"Look at this mess you've made!" she said. She yanked me from the closet and pointed to the dirty tracks on the hardwood floor. My mouth gaped open. I'd forgotten that my shoes were still covered with mud from the pigpen.

"I-I-I'm s-s-sorry, ma'am." That dreaded stutter of mine was getting worse with each passing moment. I wanted to tell her why I'd come inside, though I knew she wouldn't care. I had to tell her about Vic, but my tongue felt like it had doubled in size. The words would never come out right, and the more I stuttered, the angrier Mrs. Borg became.

"Hush your mouth with all that babbling!" she screamed. "Told that damn agency woman I didn't want any boys around here. Certainly didn't want any dummies." Her comment stung. It wasn't as if that was the first time she'd called me dumb; in fact, she said it quite frequently. That still didn't stop it from hurting my feelings.

"B-b-but, Vic," I stammered. My face was getting flushed, and I could feel the tears welling up in my eyes. Unfortunately, that was another weakness that Mrs. Borg preyed upon.

"Not only are you dumb, but you're a sissy fool. Lord, why me?" She looked up to the sky as if expecting an answer from the Lord at any moment.

I contemplated making a run for it. I didn't want to leave Vic stranded in the outhouse. I figured I was going to get whipped anyhow, so what did I have to lose? I took a deep breath, swallowing the emotion that was threatening to spill over. Mrs. Borg was still ranting at me, but her grip on my arm had loosened. I looked back into the cabinet at the roll of toilet paper that I'd managed to unwrap. If I were going to make a break for it, I'd have to be fast. With one swift motion, I snatched my arm from Mrs. Borg's grasp, grabbed the toilet paper roll, dashed around the angry woman, and burst through the door. My heart was pumping as fast as the little legs that carried me to the outhouse. It wasn't as though I thought Mrs. Borg would chase me, but the fear that came from the knowledge of what I'd just done prevented me from slowing down after I'd broken free of her. "Vic!" I called breathlessly once I was outside the door. He opened the door just enough for me to hand him the roll of paper.

"Thanks," he said after the door slammed shut again. I fell to the ground, still trying to catch my breath. I glanced expectantly at the porch and was not surprised to find Mrs. Borg standing there. The weight of her glare was like a laser, targeted right at me. Her arms were folded, and it wasn't hard to guess that she was waiting for me to come back. I sat there a moment longer, wondering how much worse the whipping would be if I prolonged going back to her. Mrs. Borg could be extremely heavy-handed when it came to whipping us. A mere switch felt more like a heavy plank smacking down on our behinds. Reluctantly, I stood up. While I didn't relish the thought of the punishment that was to come, I didn't want to run the risk of her not feeding me that day. It was only noon, and while I was sure that I had definitely run my way out of getting lunch, I figured I could still get dinner if I took my beating then.

I was just reaching the porch steps when I heard the outhouse door slam behind me. I looked over my shoulder and saw Vic walking out. His mouth dropped open when he saw Mrs. Borg standing on the porch. I turned away from him only to find that Mrs. Borg was now right in front of me. "You got nerve enough to pull away from me, huh, boy? First you dirty up my clean house, then you want to get mannish and leave while I am talking to you! Well, I've got something for you, you ungrateful little . . ."

"Wait," Vic interrupted. He'd run over to plead my case. "There wasn't any paper in the outhouse, ma'am. Ronnie was just bringing me some 'cause my stomach's been hurting awfully bad."

"Shut up!" she yelled at him. "If I want to hear something from you, I'll ask you! That's the trouble with you two, always mouthing off. You'd better get away from here, boy, and get back to your chores unless you want some of this switch too." Vic opened his mouth but then thought better of it. I could tell he didn't know what to do. Normally the threat of a whipping didn't scare him, but I imagine his backside was sore enough from all those trips to the bathroom. He gave me a sad look, as if to apologize, and then he turned toward the barn.

Mrs. Borg pulled me to the porch. Next to the hand pump was the switch that she used to whip us all the time. She grabbed it and yanked at my pants. When she'd exposed my bare bottom, she swatted me repeatedly.

"Teach you to defy me!" she exclaimed as the wiry branch smacked against my butt. I hollered in pain with each swat. Tears streamed down my face. It seemed as though she would never stop, and I wondered for the millionth time why she hated us so much. I'd only been trying to help my brother. Why couldn't she see that? Wouldn't it have been enough to make me clean up the mess I'd made? Finally, the blows stopped coming, and she released the grip she'd had on my arm. By then my cries were coming in short gasps, and it was with shaky hands that I reached to pull up my pants. "Quit all that sniveling, boy!" she grumbled. I swallowed hard, trying to compose myself quickly. I didn't want to give her a reason to hit me anymore. Once I was dressed, I swiped at my tear-stained face. I looked down at the boards on the porch, afraid to look her in the eye. After a whipping, we had to wait for her to tell us to go away before we could move. Sometimes the waiting was just as bad as the whipping itself. "Don't you defy me anymore, you hear?"

"Yes, ma'am," I said softly, thankful that my voice had been clear. There was no way that I wanted to give her a reason to yell some more.

"Get outta here," she said. l peeked up at her and watched as she disappeared into the house. I should have been relieved that it was all over, but instead I was confused. Was I supposed to go inside and clean up the footprints, or should I go back to the barn with Vic? I'd just assumed that she would tell me to come in and clean my mess, but since she hadn't, I didn't know what to do. I stood still on the porch trying to come up with the right answer. Mrs. Borg had said to stay out of the house, but at the same time, she was always after Vic and me to clean up after ourselves. After a couple seconds of contemplation, I decided that it would be best to clean up the footprints. I leaned against the hand pump and balanced on one foot to take off one shoe at a time. It was awkward trying to accomplish that, but sitting down was not an option. My butt was still stinging!

I put my shoes on the steps and quietly entered the house with my holey, sock-covered feet. I'd only taken a few steps before stopping in my tracks. Mrs. Borg was on her hands and knees cleaning the footprints I'd made. Even though I'd been careful not to slam the screen, the soft thump of the door made her look up. There were many times since I'd arrived there that I'd wished I were invisible. This was definitely one of those times. One look at me, and it was clear that her fiery anger was stoked again. "I don't believe you are in here again!" she said incredulously as she rose to her feet. She was in front of me in two quick steps. "I'll teach you," she said, snatching me again by my already sore left arm. She stormed out the door, dragging me along behind her. I had to almost run to keep from falling down, and I stumbled several times, trying to keep up with her quick pace. I think my heart was beating as fast as my legs were moving. I was nervous, wondering what she was going to do to me. We were heading toward the barn when, suddenly, she stopped in the middle of the yard near a large red brick. She abruptly let go of my arm, and my momentum made me fall to the ground. I scrambled to get up, but Mrs. Borg stopped me. "Stay down there," she grumbled. "Get on your knees right there." She pointed to the brick that was in front of me. I looked up at her, confused. What on earth was she talking about? Why did she want me to get on my knees on top of a brick? "You still want to disobey me, huh?" Her voice was sharp as she gave me a shove in the direction of the brick. "Get down there." I fell back down, surprised by her actions. My knee scraped across the rough surface of the brick, and I whimpered softly from the pain. When I was on both knees, I looked up at her. She was glaring at me, a look that I was all too familiar with. "Now, you stay right there till I say get up," she said harshly. And then, without waiting for me to answer, she turned on her heels and went back to the house. The screen door slammed closed behind her. A few minutes passed. I knelt there as I'd been told, patiently waiting for her to return. I realized that this was my punishment for coming into the house when I shouldn't have, although I figured I probably would have been punished even if I hadn't tried to come in and clean up. For Vic and me, punishment was a way of life by now. I don't think either of us went more than two days without doing something that Mrs. Borg decided deserved a few licks from her switch. More time passed, and I could feel beads of sweat forming across the top of my forehead. The sun was beating down unmercifully. I shifted a little, wondering when I would be allowed to get up. Not only were my knees beginning to feel sore, but my legs were falling asleep as well. I stared at the kitchen window, trying to see if I'd catch a glimpse of Mrs. Borg watching me, but I saw nothing. I rocked back on my heels, trying to take some of the weight off my knees. It was beginning to feel like my knees were on fire. "Straighten up!" Mrs. Borg yelled through the window. I looked up, and this time, I could see her watching me through the curtains. I straightened my back, resting my full weight on my knees. Pain shot through my legs, and I cried out.

Moments later, I heard the crunch of gravel behind me. Vic had come running from around the side of the barn to see what was going on. When he saw me, he gave me a puzzled look. "Ronnie, what are you doing?" he asked.

"Get away from there!" yelled Mrs. Borg. She had stepped back onto the porch and was waving her hands in our direction as if she were shooing flies.

"Why do you have Ronnie sitting here?" he asked. "He didn't do anything. He was just trying to help me." By that time Vic was standing right next to me. I felt a little better since he was there with me, but I had the feeling that he was going to end up getting in trouble himself.

I said, "Get away from me." Mrs. Borg had come down off the porch and was storming in our direction.

"Get out of here, Vic!" I said through clenched teeth. There was no point in both of us getting punished over some toilet paper. But Vic didn't move. He stood there defiantly and was met with a thundering backhand for his trouble. I shuddered as Vic stumbled backward from the intensity of the blow Mrs. Borg had dealt. She rarely hit us with her bare hands, so I was sure that the smack had stunned Vic just as much as it had hurt him. But when my brother fell down and didn't get up, I got worried. "Vic, get up," I called. I wanted to run to him, but Mrs. Borg was standing too close for me to even think of moving. She'd surely catch me before I could get to him. I guess she sensed my contemplation.

"Don't even think about moving, boy," she said gruffly. "Get up!" she yelled in Vic's direction. When my brother still didn't move, Mrs. Borg trudged over to him. She nudged him with a toe, but Vic lay motionless. Mrs. Borg squatted down beside him. Her eyes squinted as she looked down on him. She placed a hand on his forehead and frowned. Then she mumbled under her breath and scooped him up in her arms. When she stood up, so did I. I intended to follow her into the house. Something was wrong with my brother, and I didn't want to let him out of my sight. I was certain that this woman had done something to him, and this scared me. What would I do without Vic?

Mrs. Borg started toward the house, and I fell in step a few paces behind her. I managed to make it all the way to the porch before she realized that I was with her. She was struggling to open the screen door, so I jumped in front and pulled it open. I held it long enough for her to walk through and was about to come inside when she looked over her shoulder at me. "Just where do you think you're going? It's because of your hardheaded behind that he's like this! Now get back out there like I told you to! And this time don't move till I say so, if you know what's good for you!" I stopped dead in my tracks. This was my fault? The weight of her words caused my whole body to shake with fear. Was I really responsible for Vic's being like this? Of course I was, I concluded. If I hadn't cried out, Vic wouldn't have come running to check on me. And if he hadn't come running, Mrs. Borg wouldn't have smacked him so hard. Yes, it was my fault. I hung my head in shame and went back out to the brick. I knelt down and stared back at the house through misty eyes. Vic was my best friend, and now I'd done something to get him hurt. It was then that I knew I was truly a bad person. No wonder anybody didn't wanted me.

By the time the doctor showed up about two hours later, I was drenched with sweat. I hadn't seen Mrs. Borg since she'd gone in with Vic. I caught a glimpse of her when she came to the screen to let the doctor in. I stared in her direction, trying to get her to look my way and hoping she'd let me up. But to my dismay, she ignored me, and the two of them disappeared inside. I swallowed, trying to get rid of the thick lump in my throat, but my mouth was so dry that it didn't do much good. Several minutes later the doctor emerged from the house. When he stepped off the porch and onto the gravel road, he looked over at me. I gave him a hopeful smile, thinking that maybe he would come tell me how Vic was doing. Instead, he shook his head in what appeared to be displeasure. Obviously, he knew that this whole thing was my fault too. That made him one more person who didn't like me. Fresh tears covered my face, and I wondered why on earth I'd ever been born.

The sun had long since set, and the night air had begun to chill my damp body when Mr. Borg came out of the house to call me in for supper. By that time my legs were completely numb, and they tingled as if hundreds of needles were being pricked into them when I tried to stand.

After several attempts, I began to feel the circulation coming back to my stiff limbs, and I managed to get up. I moved slowly, feeling as though I would collapse at any moment. I hadn't eaten since breakfast, and that was hours ago. I stopped to wash my hands at the pump before going inside. There were only three place settings at the table. The missing one, of course, was Vic's. Seeing the empty space made my heart sink. Suddenly, the ravenous hunger I'd felt dissipated. When Mrs. Borg set my plate in front of me, I barely looked at it. How could I be worried about eating when I still didn't know what had happened to my brother?

Both the Borg's were eating heartily until they noticed that I hadn't so much as picked up my fork. Mr. Borg looked at me and then at Mrs. Borg. "Your brother is okay, Ronnie. He just has the flu, that's all," said Mr. Borg softly. Instantly, I perked up. The flu was something that just happened. It wasn't anything that I'd caused, and it wasn't something that Mrs. Borg had made happen to him because of me. Knowing this made me feel better. It also explained why he'd been running to the bathroom so much. I picked up my fork and dug into my meatloaf and mashed potatoes.

# Chapter 12

After Vic's bout with the flu, we received a visit from a social worker named Ms. Wilson. By that time, we'd been living with the Borg's for over a year, and the social worker was there to see how we were doing. She sat with us outside near the barn, I assumed so that we could have some privacy. She was a tall, pleasant-looking woman with an accent that we'd never heard before. When she asked us questions, it was sometimes hard to understand her, and she would have to repeat them. Thankfully, she was patient and didn't yell at us, not that I said anything anyway. Even though I wanted to tell Ms. Wilson how much I hated being with the Borg's, I was too shy to do it. The fear of not knowing what she would do with the information we gave her was enough to keep me silent. Vic, on the other hand, spouted off about everything that had happened to us. He told her about the beatings, the nights with no supper, and the awful things Mrs. Borg said to us. "She's always calling Ronnie stupid," Vic said emphatically.

"Is that true?" Ms. Wilson asked.

The sudden shift of attention in my direction caught me off guard. Throughout Vic's whole tirade against the Borg's, Ms. Wilson had only nodded and scribbled things down in her notebook. Now she was looking at me, waiting for me to corroborate what Vic had said. And of course, that was the very moment that my tongue refused to work correctly. "Y-y-yes," I stammered. Ms. Wilson stared at me for a moment and then scribbled some more in her notebook. When she looked up at me again, she shook her head slightly and frowned. I felt my face grow hot. The expression on her face was clear to me. She thought I was stupid too. After that, she talked to us for only a few more minutes before going in to talk to Mr. and Mrs. Borg. Vic and I sat outside on the porch and waited. My stomach pitched with anxiety. I wondered how much Ms. Wilson would tell them about what Vic had said. Of course, it really didn't matter. Any of it was enough to get us in trouble. I was thinking about what our punishment might be when something totally unexpected happened.

"Come on in here, boys."

The sound of Mrs. Borg's voice calling us into the house startled us both. We weren't usually allowed inside until suppertime, for one thing, and the tone of her voice was much too pleasant, for another. I looked at Vic quizzically, but he just shrugged his shoulders. He was as surprised as I was. "Well, come on," Mrs. Borg called again. This time she was standing right in front of the screen door. In her hand was a large plate with cookies piled on it.

Vic stood up slowly, looking puzzled. I didn't move, though. I wasn't sure what to make of her sudden change of demeanor, but I didn't trust it. "Ronnie, don't you want any of my cookies?" she asked sweetly. My jaw dropped. She was offering us cookies? We were hardly ever given anything sweet. Mrs. Borg didn't normally bake unless it was a special occasion, and sometimes not even then. But now here she was offering us cookies. Was this some sort of trick? I sniffed the sweet smell of the freshly baked cookies. If it was a trick, I didn't care. I jumped up from the stairs and went inside with my brother.

Ms. Wilson was sitting at the table talking with Mr. Borg when we walked in. When she heard the scuffing sound of our boots, she stopped midsentence and looked over at us. "It seems that things are going just fine here," she said, closing her notebook. "You boys are very lucky to have the Borg's." She shot a scolding look in each of our directions. It wasn't at all hard to figure out what it meant. Nothing we'd told her mattered. It was obvious that the Borg's had disposed of any accusations we had made. Suddenly, the cookie in my mouth tasted more like a dry piece of cardboard instead of a treat. No doubt about it, Vic and I were in for it as soon as Ms. Wilson left.

"Thank you both for being so hospitable," Ms. Wilson gushed as she took another cookie. She stood to leave, and Mrs. Borg walked with her to the door. As soon as the two women left the room, Mr. Borg got up and went to his bedroom to get ready for work.

"Now what?" I asked when Vic and I were alone at the table. "You know we're going to get it." At first, Vic didn't answer. In fact, he didn't even look as if he'd heard me. Next thing I knew, he jumped up from the table and dashed to the screen door. I watched him peek outside and then come streaking back into the dining room.

"Take some of those cookies and come on," he said hurriedly.

"Huh?" What in the world was wrong with him? He had to know that those cookies weren't really meant for us.

"Grab some of those cookies," he hissed. "Hurry up!" The urgency in his voice made me hop up from my seat and do what he said. He was grabbing handfuls of the cookies and stuffing them into a pouch that he'd made by lifting the tail end of his shirt. Though I didn't know how Vic figured we were going to get away with this, I followed suit.

"That's enough," he whispered. "Follow me." Vic took off for the stairs, and it was then that I realized what his plan was. We were going to stash the cookies in our room. Vic scanned the room for a good hiding place.

"What about in there?" I asked, pointing my toe at the black duffel bag that was halfway under the bed.

"Yeah, that's good," he said. We dumped the cookies in the bag hurriedly, dropping several of them in the process. When we finished, we did our best to scatter the crumbs around so they couldn't be seen.

"We'd better get back downstairs," I said nervously. I could just imagine Mrs. Borg sneaking upstairs and catching us. The thought of the type of whipping that would bring made me shudder. We clumped quickly back down the stairs, our boots making far too much noise, but we didn't have time to be concerned about that. We were more interested in saving our butts.

Mrs. Borg's heavy footsteps, followed by the squeaking sound of the opening screen door, met us as we slid into our seats. Seconds later, she appeared in the dining room. All traces of any smile on her face had been replaced with that scowl Vic and I had grown accustomed to. Things were back to normal now.

"What are you still sitting here for?" she snarled. "Don't you have chores to tend to?"

Neither of us said a word. It wasn't as if Mrs. Borg really wanted an answer from us. What she wanted was for us to get out of the house, which is what we got up to do. We were only a few steps from the safety of the outdoors when her voice thundered behind us.

"You gluttons ate all those cookies!"

We both froze momentarily and then bolted through the door. It was certain that Mrs. Borg would get us for taking the cookies and leaving while she was talking to us, but we'd deal with that later in the evening. Once inside the barn, we climbed up into the loft and flopped down on the scattered hay. My heart was still racing from running so fast, and I lay there breathing heavily. When Vic started laughing, I sat up and looked at him. "Can you imagine what her face looked like when she saw all those cookies gone?" he asked in between chuckles. I thought about it for a moment and then burst into a fit of laughter as well. Mrs. Borg was probably fuming. It had no doubt been extremely hard for her to pretend to be nice to us for the duration of Ms. Wilson's visit, especially since she didn't have much practice in doing so. I was willing to bet that even Mr. Borg was surprised by her act, although he didn't show it. Mr. Borg didn't show emotion about too much of anything. We barely saw him. He was either at work or sleeping to get ready to go to work. When he wasn't getting ready for work, he was in the field until suppertime. And then when we saw him at suppertime, he didn't really say much. I wondered what he thought about how Mrs. Borg treated us.

"Hey, Vic, do you think Mr. Borg ever says anything to her about how mean she is?" I asked. Even though I doubted that he did, I wanted to know what my brother thought.

"No," he said after a second of contemplation. "He probably doesn't get a chance to say much. He probably doesn't care about us anyhow. Why should he?" Vic got up. "Forget them."

He walked over and grabbed onto a rope that was hanging from the rafters. "Bet you I can make it across to the other side," he said.

"No, you can't," I said with a smile. We'd been trying to reach the other loft by swinging across on that rope for months. So far, neither of us had succeeded in making it, but of the two of us, I had come the closest.

"Yeah, I can," he said. He pushed off from the edge of the platform and swung through the air. I held my breath as I watched him hurtle toward the other side. But he didn't have enough momentum, and the rope stopped way short of the next platform. His body began to swing back to where I was standing.

"Ha!" I exclaimed tauntingly. "You didn't even get close." Vic landed back on the platform and passed me the rope.

"Here, you still can't do it either," he challenged. With a cocky smile, I grabbed the rope and carefully positioned it between my legs. I took a few extra steps backward for a running start and then sailed off the platform. I was going to do it this time; I could feel it. The rafter groaned from the pull of the rope as it propelled me through the air. The edge of the platform was almost within my reach, so I unwrapped my legs from around the rope. My success wouldn't count if I made it to the other side but didn't manage to get off the rope. Because I'd never gotten quite this close before, I had never unwrapped my legs before. And because of that, I had no idea how many my legs were a part of what kept me up on that rope. My dangling legs felt heavy, and my hands began to slip. Panic ran through me, and I flailed my legs wildly, trying to get my footing onto the platform, but the idea backfired. All the wiggling of my body disrupted the natural swinging of the rope, and instead of continuing toward the other side, the rope began to swing from side to side, and my momentum slowed down. I pumped my legs, trying to keep from stopping, but the rope continued to slow down. By then I was swinging back and forth like a pendulum, not slow enough to jump off but not fast enough to reach either side of the loft.

"Help me, Vic!" I yelled. When I looked down, the ground seemed extremely far away. I had no idea how I was going to get off the rope, and by then, I desperately wanted off.

"Hang on, Ronnie!" he called as he scrambled down the ladder. In a flash, he was standing below me on the barn floor, trying to grab the end of the rope. Unfortunately, he was too short and he couldn't reach it. Fear gripped me, and my hands started to perspire. I slipped a few more inches.

"Hurry, Vic!" My voice wavered, and I was on the verge of tears. If he didn't figure out how to get me down soon, I was going to fall. And then, just as I thought that, my hands slid even further, and for the first time, I felt the slicing burn of the rope go through my hands. There was only a few feet of rope left for me to hold on to.

"Pull yourself up, Ronnie," Vic said. On the ground, he still obviously had not figured out how to get me down because he was running back and forth beneath me. I struggled with the rope while trying to inch my legs upward. But as soon as I let go with one hand, the other hand slid down the rope, and I plummeted to the ground.

When I finally opened my eyes, Mrs. Borg was standing over me, muttering under her breath. I blinked and then squeezed my eyes shut. My head ached terribly, and my face felt hot. I wanted to get up, but it was too difficult. My body wouldn't cooperate. I closed my eyes again, and everything faded to black. Vic was grinning down at me when I woke up again. This time I was lying in my bed. My head was still throbbing but not as bad as it had been earlier. "You got a big knot on your head," Vic said, still smiling. Immediately I reached for the back of my head. There was indeed a large lump on the back of my head. I winced when my hand touched it. It hurt something awful. I wiggled the rest of my body. Arms, legs, hands—everything else seemed to be okay. Luckily, I had fallen on a bed of hay. But why did my head hurt so much? "The doctor was here," Vic volunteered. "He said you got a concussion." Vic seemed proud of my battle scar, which meant that Mrs. Borg was probably furious. I struggled to get up, but a sharp wave of pain shot through my head, and I collapsed back down on my pillow.

"Ouch!" I squeezed my eyes shut to keep from crying.

"You got to lay down for a couple of days," Vic said solemnly. "The doctor said." A couple of days seemed like a long time. I couldn't imagine having to stay in the house that long, nor could I believe that Mrs. Borg was at all pleased about it. Besides, with me in bed, that would mean that Vic had to do all the chores by himself. It was hard enough for us to finish them together. Doing them alone would be almost impossible.

"But I got to help you," I protested halfheartedly. The throbbing in my head was returning, and with each movement it began to get worse.

"It's okay," he said. "I can do it by myself." The sound of footsteps coming up the stairs quieted us both. They weren't heavy, so we knew it wasn't Mrs. Borg. Our eyes were glued to the door as we waited to see who was coming. It was Mr. Borg.

"Vic," he said quietly, "come on so we can get these chores out of the way." He looked at me briefly. "How're you feeling, Ronnie?"

"My head hurts," I answered.

"I'll bet it does," he said, smiling a little. "That was quite a fall you had. You boys have got to be more careful. I can't take off from work anymore for things like this." His tone changed a little when he said that. It wasn't quite as friendly as it had been, but it wasn't angry either. It was hard to tell if he was upset, especially since he hardly ever spoke to us. "Let's go, Vic." The two of them turned and walked away. Vic looked back at me over his shoulder and smiled.

# Chapter 13

Before we knew it, we had been with the Borg's for five years. Both Vic and I were in school, and though it provided an escape from Mrs. Borg's constant nagging, it wasn't a pleasant experience either. Almost from day one, the kids teased me about one thing or another. My clothes, the way we smelled, my speech—it was always something. It got to the point that I couldn't stand to be in either place. The day came when I'd finally had enough.

It had been a typical morning. Vic and I arose early to do some of our chores before going to school. We fed the chickens, collected eggs, and slopped the pigs as usual, and we left the other tasks for when we returned. We were getting ready to get on the road to walk to school when Mrs. Borg stopped us. "I'm going into town, so you two can hop on the tractor with me." I groaned inwardly. Even though the walk to school was a long one, it still beat riding on the back of that dirty tractor. I hated it because it got our clothes so dusty, and it seemed to always leave us smelling like the animals. And of course, that was one of the main reasons that we were always being teased.

"We can walk, ma'am," I said, looking at Vic to back me up. I knew that speaking up was likely to spark her anger, but it didn't matter. There were times when her yelling didn't seem to compare to the cruelty of the kids at school.

"I don't need you to tell me what you can do," she said stonily. "I told the two of you to come on with me."

I thought for a moment, wondering if it would be worth it to anger her further and risk a spanking. Just when I was coming to the conclusion that it might be worth it, Vic tugged me by my arm. "C'mon, Ronnie," he said. I pulled my arm away. Vic looked at me strangely and then turned away to follow Mrs. Borg. I stood there, upset with Vic for not taking my side. Even though he didn't have quite as hard a time fitting in at school as I did, I thought he would at least stick with me. I sighed and walked slowly to the tractor. When we arrived in front of the school, there were a bunch of kids playing together, waiting for the bell to ring. The loud, rattling sound of the tractor made them stop what they were doing and look in our direction. As soon as Vic and I climbed down, the kids began snickering and pointing. I hung my head and headed straight for the classroom. Any chance I'd had of getting in on a game of tag had been ruined by a tractor ride.

Soon after we arrived, the bell rang, and the rest of the kids in my class trooped in. A few of them continued to giggle as they passed me, while others made sniffing sounds. I shrunk down further in my seat. Every day I wished I could become invisible, but I hadn't been able to do it so far. So until I was able to completely disappear, sinking down into my seat as far as I could was the best I could do.

On most days, our lessons started with math, but on this particular morning, our teacher, Mrs. King, decided to change the schedule. She told us to pull out our reading books and then began choosing students to read aloud. I was chosen to read second. As if my day weren't already going badly enough, this was certain to make it worse. My heart was pounding so hard that I thought I could feel it coming out of my chest. I waited my turn, praying that some miracle would happen that would keep me from stuttering. But of course, I knew that miracles didn't happen, at least not for me, so I prayed for a distraction that would keep me from having to take my turn. Neither of those things happened, and once my classmate Margaret finished reading, Mrs. King moved in front of me. "Ronnie, please read the next three paragraphs." I took a deep breath and stared down at the page. The words glared out at me, and my heartbeat thundered in my ears. I tried to swallow, but my mouth was so dry that it didn't do much good. After another deep breath, I opened my mouth and started reading the words on the page. At first my words came out clearly, which was a shock to me. But by the middle of the first paragraph, I began to stumble over the words, and my face became flush.

"Told you he was a dummy," whispered one of the boys a few seats over.

"Why does he even come to school?" someone else asked. Tears welled up in my eyes against my will. I stopped trying to read and wiped at them quickly. I was called so many different names that I didn't want them to add "crybaby" to the list. Snickers sputtered through the room, and Mrs. King quickly hushed them. She gave me a sympathetic look and moved to the next student.

By lunchtime, I had had enough of school and the Borg's. Since none of the kids paid any attention to me anyway, it was easy to slip behind a tree and out of the school yard without being seen. I trudged down the dusty trail toward town. I had no idea where I was going, but it didn't matter. As far as I was concerned, anywhere was better than where I had been. After about thirty minutes of walking, I started to feel bad about leaving Vic behind. The feeling quickly subsided when I thought of how he'd treated me earlier that morning. If only he'd decided to walk with me, maybe the day wouldn't have been quite as bad. When I reached town, I didn't know what to do. The sun was beating down on me, and my throat was parched. By that time, I knew that school was over and that Vic was probably wondering where I was. I figured he'd look for me for a while before leaving. I thought about what Mrs. Borg would say once he got home without me. Most likely she'd scream at him, but I hoped that she wouldn't spank him because of me. I walked around town, avoiding the looks of grown-ups. Occasionally, I stopped and peered inside the large store windows. It was getting later and later, and pretty soon my stomach grumbled hungrily. The sun was sinking, and I imagined that Vic was just about finished with the chores. It was almost suppertime, and I had no idea as to what I would eat. For that matter, I didn't even know where I would sleep. Several hours had passed since I had left school, and I was very tired and very hungry. The town was fairly small, and I had walked around the same area more times than I could count. As I was approaching the grocery store again, I decided to sit down and rest. There was a stoop near the entrance, and I plopped down on it wearily. Men and women looked at me curiously as they entered and exited the store. I didn't recognize any of them, and that disappointed me. Perhaps if I could find someone who knew the Borg's, they would feel sorry enough for me that they would take me home with them. Another hour passed. The wind started to bite, and I was close to tears. An elderly woman came out of the store and stood in front of me.

"Are your parents in the store?" she asked.

I shook my head sadly. "No, ma'am."

"Well, where are they?" she asked curiously.

"At home," I said, quietly.

"Well, then, you should go home," she said sternly.

Her tone was crisp and almost as icy as the wind that had started to pick up as night fell. My tears fell hot but cooled on my cheeks when the air hit them. I shivered. As much as I didn't want to agree, the old woman was right. I had nowhere to go, and during times like these, it was ridiculous for me to think that someone else would take me home with them. The reality was that I had no choice but to go back to the Borg's. I stood up, stepped down off the stoop, and began the long walk home.

By the time I got back to the farm, it was very late. For some reason it surprised me that neither Mr. nor Mrs. Borg were on the road looking for me. Instead, the house was dark. I walked onto the porch and pulled on the screen door, praying that it wouldn't squeak. Even though I knew I wouldn't avoid punishment, I hoped to at least delay it until morning. At that moment, I was exhausted and only wanted to sleep.

Despite my caution, the door squeaked noisily. I winced and then waited. I expected Mrs. Borg to come fling the door open, breathing fire, at any moment. When nothing happened after a few seconds, I reached for the doorknob. It wouldn't turn. The door was locked. My heart sank. I slid down to the floor and burst into tears. I was cold, tired, and hungry, and now I was locked out of the house. I got up slowly and tried to close the screen quietly. Just as I was about to walk off the porch, the front door creaked open. I stopped, sure that I was dead.

"Ronnie!"

At the sound of Vic's whisper, I spun around. I couldn't remember a time that I was happier to see him. "C'mon," he whispered urgently. I smiled weakly and hurried through the screen door. The two of us moved quickly and quietly up the stairs, avoiding the creaky boards. When we got into our room, Vic looked at me angrily.

"Where'd you go?"

I shook my head sadly. I didn't want to talk about where I had been, at least not right then since I couldn't eat. I simply wanted to sleep. I peeled off my clothes and hopped into bed. Vic was still standing in the middle of the room, staring at me. "Please don't be mad, Vic," I said desperately. He frowned for a second and then grinned at me.

"Hungry?" he asked. I bobbed my head up and down vigorously. I should have known that I could count on Vic to save me something. I watched as he went to one of the dresser drawers. He reached under the clothes and came out with something wrapped in a towel. My stomach growled violently as the smell of what was inside began to permeate through the layers of the towel. Finally, he unveiled a thick pork chop. I looked at him in disbelief. I couldn't imagine how he'd managed to sneak something so big off the table. Over the years, we had gotten good at saving food from dinner and sneaking it to our rooms for later. But it had always been small things, like biscuits or, occasionally, a chicken leg. However he'd been able to do it didn't matter, though. I thankfully accepted the food from my brother and took a huge bite.

"What was it like?" Vic asked curiously.

I chewed thoughtfully. "It was terrible," I said finally. "There was nothing to do but wander around. People looked at me funny."

"I didn't think you were coming back," he said, sounding worried. "Mrs. Borg was really mad!" Vic chuckled. "She was screaming about how ungrateful we were and that she didn't care if you came back or not." My eyes widened. If Mrs. Borg had felt that way, I wondered how she would react when she saw me in the morning—that is, of course, after she spanked me first. Maybe she would call the agency and they would take me away. The idea of that didn't seem so bad, but then I began to think. What if they sent me away without Vic? That saddened me. Just because I had left school by myself didn't mean I wanted to be somewhere else without Vic. I finished my pork chop and settled down to go to sleep. My punishment would come at the crack of dawn. I just hoped that it wouldn't include being away from my brother.

Despite my desire to stay with my brother, my unhappiness at the Borg's' house caused me to hit the road several more times over the next two years. It usually happened after a disheartening visit from one of the social workers. Vic and I would complain about the way we were treated, and the social workers would ignore us. They were always reminding us that we were lucky to have found a home and that there were dozens of children who hadn't been so fortunate. After each visit, things got worse for about a week. It seemed that Mrs. Borg became angry with us for just being around. Everything we did was wrong, and the beatings came more frequently. Several times, I took some clothes and food we stashed from dinner and disappeared into the night. As usual, I didn't have much of a plan, so I ended up returning to face the music. It was a cycle that went on and on, seemingly without an end. We were stuck with the Borg's, and there wasn't a thing we could do about it.

# Chapter 14

I had just about given up praying for things to change when, very abruptly, they did. Vic was thirteen, and I was twelve. Eight years had passed since we had arrived at the Borg's, and surprisingly we had found a way to survive. It was a Saturday afternoon, and Vic and I were dragging freshly bundled bales of hay into the barn. Mr. Borg was driving the tractor in the field, and "the horrible Mrs.", which was what we now called Mrs. Borg, was somewhere in the house. The heat was boring down on us, and as soon as we finished with the last bale, Vic and I collapsed on the barn floor.

"You want to play horseshoes later?" I asked Vic as I stared up into the rafters. We usually played once we finished our chores. I had gotten good over the last year, and it had become much harder for Vic to beat me.

"Yeah, sure," he said, chewing on a piece of hay.

I looked over at my brother. There was a scowl on his face, as if he were deep in thought over something. I was just about to ask him what was on his mind when a loud scream rang out. The two of us scrambled toward the sound of the anguished cries. It was coming from out in the field. We ran swiftly in that direction, nearly colliding with Mrs. Borg, who had come running from inside the house. As we got closer, we could hear the tractor motor. It was making a grinding sound that sputtered at intervals and mixed horribly with Mr. Borg's screams.

We all reached him at the same time, and the sight staggered me. Blood was everywhere. Mr. Borg lay on the ground, his leg a tattered mess beneath the teeth of the huge tractor. The teeth spun and then halted, which explained the grinding sound we'd heard. I watched, paralyzed. Vic passed by me and hopped onto the tractor. He killed the engine, and Mrs. Borg raced over to her husband. "Go to the neighbors', quick!" she cried over her shoulder. I didn't move. I couldn't. I'd never seen so much human blood in my life. And to see Mr. Borg on the ground writhing in pain scared me.

"Go, Ronnie!" said Vic. He had gotten off the tractor and nudged me in the direction of the road, and then he rushed over to help Mrs. Borg. After one more glance at them, I took off like a shot. I sprinted down the driveway and onto the dirt road. The closest neighbor was a little over a mile away, but I made it in record time. When I got there, I banged loudly on the door. A few minutes later, Mr. Peters came from around the side of the house.

"What on earth are you doing, boy?" he asked, his voice filled with annoyance.

"Come quick," I said breathlessly. "Mr. Borg's been hurt."

"What?" Mr. Peters threw down his rake and hurried over to me.

"The tractor," I gulped air. "His leg . . ."

"C'mon, boy," he said, grabbing me by the arm.

We spent the next few weeks at the Petersen' house while Mr. Borg was in the hospital. Before and after school, we were required to go to the farm and do our regular chores and then any chores that Mr. Peters had for us. Needless to say, we were exhausted every night, but the situation was an improvement from being at the Borg's. I secretly wished we wouldn't have to go back. Though the Petersen weren't overly nice, they were much more pleasant to be around, and they didn't yell the way Mrs. Borg did. In fact, Mr. Peters sometimes played horseshoes with us. It was a strange, yet nice, change to hear the voice of a man around the house. While Mr. Borg rarely spoke, Mr. Peters talked incessantly. He was a know-it-all who always inserted his opinion about everything. Regretfully, the day for our return to the Borg's' house came. It was late in the evening when Mr. Peters drove us there. He parked in front of the house, and we all just sat there for a few minutes. None of us was sure what to expect. Mrs. Peters had told us a few days earlier that the tractor had done so much damage to Mr. Borg's leg that the doctor had had to amputate it. I had spent most of the night before trying to imagine what that would look like. I had never known that a person could manage with one leg, let alone seen anyone like that.

"Let's go," said Mr. Peters.

Mrs. Borg must have heard the slamming of the truck doors because she was at the front door before we stepped onto the porch. We hadn't seen her the entire time that we'd been gone, and somehow she looked different. Her face was drawn, and she was a little thinner. The only things that hadn't changed were her mean expression and her ugly disposition. We were barely inside before she began growling a bunch of do's and don'ts at us.

"Keep quiet, and don't go asking a bunch of questions! And don't stare at him!"

Neither of us said a word; we only nodded our heads. Since she'd already told us to keep quiet, we saw no need to verbalize our understanding of her instructions. We were certain that the less talking we did the better. She looked us over, contemplating whether or not she needed to bark at us anymore.

Once she was sure we understood her, she smiled at Mr. Peters and led us into their bedroom. Mr. Borg had never been a very large man. In fact, compared to his wife, he was somewhat dwarfed. From first glance, it was obvious that during his stay at the hospital, Mr. Borg had also lost weight. He was pale and looked as though he had aged tremendously in the weeks since we'd seen him last.

Mr. Peters walked right up alongside the bed and sat in a chair that was there. Vic and I hung back by the door and watched as the two men talked. Thankfully, Mrs. Borg had gone to the kitchen right after she'd ushered us to the bedroom. With her out of the way, we were able to study Mr. Borg without fear of reprimand. But there wasn't really much to see. His body was concealed under the covers, so we couldn't see the space where his leg used to be. I wasn't quite sure I wanted to see it anyway.

"Boys, come on in." Mr. Borg beckoned us over.

We both hung back at first, waiting for the other to take the first step. But after seeing that I wasn't going to budge, Vic walked slowly over to the bed. I followed, reluctantly. "Mr. Peters tells me the two of you were a big help to him on his farm," he said. "I am glad you earned your keep. Going to be a lot of things need doing back here. Mr. Peters is going to come over and help with some of the field work. That means no goofing off in the barn." He looked directly at me when he said it.

"Yes, sir," we said in unison.

"Good. Now you two go on out of here while I finished talking to Mr. Peters." I hurried out of the room first. His dismissal came not a moment too soon. I had begun to feel uncomfortable when I saw Mr. Borg's good leg shifting under the cover while he spoke. It was then that I noticed the differences in the length of each leg. I shuddered to think of what it actually looked like underneath. I was in such a rush to get out of there that I nearly knocked Mrs. Borg over.

"Watch it, boy," she grumbled.

"Sorry," I muttered, dodging out of her way. I took the stairs two at a time and retreated to my room. I flopped down on the bed. Vic came in a few minutes later.

"Pretty weird, huh?" he said.

"Yeah," I answered quietly. "He's not ever going to be able to do anything on the farm again."

Vic sighed. "Yeah, and we both know what that means." I didn't say anything, but I didn't have to. The weight of running the farm was going to fall on our shoulders, and like most everything else in our lives, we had no control over it. In the months that followed, Vic and I all but gave up going to school. Our chores almost tripled. Just like Mr. Borg had said, Mr. Peters came over to help us with plowing the field, but that proved to be short-lived. After two trips, he quickly decided that the added work was more than he was willing to take on.

"Sorry, boys," he said one afternoon. "I've got my own farm to tend to, and it takes 'bout a full day just to plow yours. You two are going to have to do it yourselves." And just like that, he stopped coming over. He didn't bother to show us how to do the plowing or anything. Naturally, Mrs. Borg assumed that his absence had to do with something we'd done wrong. She ignored us when we tried to tell her what he'd said. "Hush your mouths," she hissed. "You lazy, no-account, good-for-nothings done run off the only help we had. Look at my field!" In the two short weeks since Mr. Peters had stopped coming by, the field had grown almost as tall as we were. I could understand why Mrs. Borg was upset, at least about the way the field looked. But it still bothered me that she never believed anything we told her. "Get out there and cut that field."

"But . . ." sputtered Vic.

"Don't give me any lip," she said, cutting him off midsentence. So we trudged off to try to make heads or tails of the task that lay before us. It took us the entire day to finish, and when we were done, we were exhausted but somewhat proud of ourselves. Though it didn't look like one of the men had done it, we hadn't completely butchered it, either. Needless to say, Mrs. Borg pointed out all that was wrong with it that first time, but after a few weeks, we mastered it, and her complaints stopped.

"I said I want another drink!" The shouting and the crash of glass against the wall woke Vic and me instantly. Each of us sat straight up in bed and rubbed our eyes. We sat there listening as the yelling below us continued. Mr. Borg was drunk again. That was obvious by the slurring of his words when he spoke.

"And I said that you don't need another drink!" Mrs. Borg screamed.

"Awe, man," Vic groaned. "They're going to keep us up again." He flopped back down on his pillow and covered his ears. I sighed loudly and lay back down too. For the previous few months, the fighting between the Borg's had become a nightly occurrence. Mr. Borg usually got up in the morning and hopped around on his crutches, getting in Mrs. Borg's way. After breakfast, he would begin drinking and pretty much continue throughout the day. Since his accident, he had transformed into an evil, bitter man who yelled obscenities at anybody who looked at him for too long. He was nothing like the quiet man we'd met when we first came to the farm. As if one screaming adult hadn't been enough, now Vic and I had to deal with two.

"Woman, if I say get me a drink, I mean it!" he shouted.

"Shut up you old, one-legged drunk!"

Vic sat up again, his jaw dropped with surprise. I raised my eyebrows. In all the arguments we'd overheard, Mrs. Borg had never mentioned Mr. Borg's having one leg. In fact, she had whipped Vic something terrible for making the mistake of asking Mr. Borg how it felt to have only one leg.

All of the sudden, everything was quiet. Vic and I strained to hear what was going on. It was hard to believe that Mr. Borg had not exploded over his wife's comments. Just when I was beginning to think that it was safe to go back to sleep, we heard the unmistakable click of Mr. Borg's shotgun.

"One-legged drunk?" shouted Mr. Borg. "Woman, I'll kill you!"

The two of us shot up like rockets. We flew down the stairs and saw Mr. Borg standing near the sofa, leaning on his crutch. He had his gun in hand, aimed directly at a very scared Mrs. Borg. She stood motionless near the old radio. Her face was pale, her eyes full of fear. When she heard us come downstairs, she skirted a look in our direction, but she didn't say anything. I think that was the first time I'd ever seen her speechless. Mr. Borg didn't pay any attention to us. His anger was trained on his wife, and that worked to our advantage. Both Vic and I bolted off the stairs and through the screen door into the night air. We'd moved so fast that I am sure we must have looked like a blur to both the Borg's. Our feet barely hit the dirt road as we continued to run down the driveway in the direction of the Petersen' house. By the time we reached their house, we were breathless. Vic and I pounded our fists against the front door. "What on earth is wrong with you boys?" Mrs. Peters asked as she pulled her robe tight around her. Mr. Peters appeared behind her, holding his own shotgun. When he saw that it was only us, he leaned it up against the door frame and looked at us curiously.

"What's going on, boys? What are you doing out here this time of night?" he asked.

"It's Mr. Borg," Vic began.

"He says he's going to kill Mrs. Borg," I finished.

"Oh, my Lord!" Mrs. Peters exclaimed. She turned to her husband. "You'd better get over there." Mr. Peters grabbed his coat from the rack near the door and hurried onto the porch. He was halfway down the steps when he stopped and turned back. He reached inside the door, past his wife, and snatched up his shotgun. Mrs. Peters gave him an alarmed look.

"If he's liquored up, I might need this," he said somberly. "No telling what that crazy fool might do."

Vic and I looked at each other. As unpredictable as Mr. Borg had been lately, the possibility of his actually shooting someone suddenly became very real. We rushed to the passenger side of Mr. Peters's truck and slid onto the cool, vinyl seat. He turned the ignition, and the truck coughed loudly in the chilly night air. After a few sputtering attempts, the engine roared to life. Mr. Peters popped the gear in drive, and we sped down the road, leaving a cloud of dust behind us.

It surprised me to find the Borg's standing in the same spots that we'd left them in. I guessed we'd been gone at least fifteen minutes, yet Mrs. Borg was still glued near the radio. Her husband was still aiming his shotgun at her. Mr. Peters marched noisily onto the porch, but Vic and I hung back. We had no intention of returning inside that house until all the guns were put away. In his current state, there was no telling what Mr. Borg might do, and we couldn't be sure that his anger wouldn't be sparked by Mr. Peters's arrival.

"Art, put that thing away," said Mr. Peters harshly.

At first I was a little confused. Who in the world was Art? And then I realized that Mr. Peters was talking to Mr. Borg. It may sound ridiculous, but in all our years with the Borg's, we'd never heard anyone call them by their first names.

"Told that woman to fix me a drink," Mr. Borg said stubbornly. "She keeps sassing me, calling me a drunk. I ought to kill her. Bet that'd shut her up, eh?" He chuckled, as if amused by the thought of shutting his wife up. I covered my face with my hands. If he was going to do it, I definitely didn't want to see it.

"No, Art," said Mr. Peters patiently. "You should not kill her. That's you're wife, and murder is bad anyhow. Now let me hold that gun." He held his hand out. Mr. Borg eyed him suspiciously.

"How come you want my gun, and you're holding one in your hand?" I held my breath. I wanted this entire scene to be over without incident, but Mr. Borg didn't seem willing to cooperate. Chills ran through me, and I couldn't help feeling fearful that Mr. Borg would indeed shoot someone. But then he seemed to have a change of heart. Surprisingly, he lowered his gun and passed it to Mr. Peters. He looked at him and then at his wife. "She isn't worth it anyway. I'll get my own drink." He pulled his other crutch under his arm and took a step forward. His body swayed a little, and he took another step. The third step sent him crashing to the floor. The two grown-ups rushed over to him to help him up, but he was already passed out.

Another social worker showed up the very next morning. I doubt that it was by coincidence. More than likely, Mrs. Peters had contacted the agency after the previous night's events. Vic and I had opted to sleep out in the barn even though Mr. Borg was out cold. We knew it wasn't likely that he'd wake up again before the morning, but it was sure better to be safe than sorry.

Since the visit was a surprise, Mrs. Borg had no way of denying the reports that the social worker had received. There was still broken glass on the floor in the living room, and the house was in general disarray. Aside from that, Mr. Borg was still feeling mean-spirited and was definitely not on his best behavior. The social worker didn't even bother to ask us how things were going. Instead, she told us to go upstairs and pack all of our belongings. Three jaws dropped open—mine, Vic's, and Mrs. Borg's. When her words actually registered, Vic and I took off up the stairs. Clothes were shoved haphazardly into the black bag that we'd arrived with, and everything that didn't fit, we piled into our arms. We wasted no time and were clumping back down the stairs in a flash. We didn't want Mrs. Borg to have the opportunity to change the social worker's mind about taking us away. And that is exactly what she was trying to do when we made it back to the living room. "But who will help with the field?" she whined. I stopped in my tracks. *Please don't let her change her mind,* I prayed. My heart was in my throat while I waited for the woman to answer.

"That's not my problem," the social worker said with a shrug. "Come on, boys. I have just the place for you."

It wasn't until the blue Chrysler began to roll down the driveway that I really believed we were leaving the Borg's. After years of wishing, hoping, and praying, it had finally come true. I turned in my seat and watched from the rear window as the farm, the animals, and Mrs. Borg's permanent scowl faded into a cloud of dust.

Red Cross entry dated February 26, 1946:

> This needful boy is quick to say he is not wanted and has stated so regarding his foster home and school settings. Without a doubt, according to his interpretations, there is merit to what Ronald says objectively, as well as normal exchange expected may become tiresome or exhausting to school staff and peer groups. A slight cession of the amount previously extended may be easily interpreted by Ronald

as being rejected as well as not being wanted. Ronald does not like his foster mother and wants to be replaced even "if I have to go to an orphanage." His main reasons are that his foster mother doesn't want him; she is always yelling at him and is too bossy. Other reasons are that he is tired of being isolated on a farm as he can't go anywhere or do anything or make friends easily. Realistically, the farm is in semi-isolation regarding proximity to the nearby community as well as it being true that the use of the family car is limited since Mr. Borg drives to work. Otherwise, Ronald is saying that his total needs have not been met, which is true. Ronald is an appealing 12-year-old boy with dark brown hair, brown eyes, and a medium-sized build. He is very likable and relates quickly to those he feels are interested in him. Ronald is very sensitive and responds rapidly to positive and negative feelings transferred to him. His reaction to positive feelings is shown in a display of elative smiling, where his reaction to negative transfer feelings is exhibited by passive withdrawal and hurt expressions on his face. Ronald is more prone to withholding his embittered feelings, sulking as well as feeling self-pity rather than expressing and the release of what is bothering him. Most of his relationships are superficial, and some are manipulative. He will buy love, affection, and attention through manipulation if his physical appeal does not elicit his needs to be gratified. At one time, he stole 20 dollars from his foster mother and gave dollar bills out at school in his endeavor to purchase friendship. Early childhood symptoms of disturbance such as enuresis, stealing, tantrums, passive withdrawing, and nonconformity have subsided considerably in submerged repressive and suppressive states. Light volcanic eruptions occur occasionally when unconscious control devices break down from an over flooding of withdrawal and withholding mechanisms. Ronald will reverse his mechanistic operating defenses and reveal part of his basic self and feelings by becoming aggressively hostile and demanding. The action taken away may be directed at himself by further withdrawal and self-pity or at others by exhibiting his temper. On several occasions during these states, he has threatened to run away from his foster home (at the Borg's), hence getting back at his foster mother. Unfortunately, Mrs. Borg's personality structure makes it difficult for Ronald to receive the love, affection, and attention he needs. She is masculinity inclined and feels more comfortable with a child who is the tough and rough type. Interpretatively speaking, she is not prepared because of a lacking in her early life to give Ronald attention and affection. Ronald's earlier bids for love and affection were interpreted by Mrs. Borg as being sissified and effeminate. She therefore used to "shoo him" him outside to rough and tough him up with Victor. Instead of love and attention, Ronald received rejection.

# Chapter 15

"First one finishes three laps gets to have the loser make his bed for a whole week." Charles was always making bets, but this was one that I was certain he would lose. I'd become quite the swimmer in the four years that I'd been at the Illinois Soldiers and Sailors Children's Home, and very few boys had the nerve to challenge me in that area. But Charles was new, so he didn't know better yet. I fully intended to teach him. It would be nice to not have to worry about making my bed for a week.

The ISSC had been home to Vic and me since we left the Borg's' farm. It was a large area of land that consisted of several white cottages, a school, a gymnasium, a recreation room, and the indoor pool that I was swimming in. When we'd first arrived, I'd been pretty skeptical. There were so many kids there that it reminded me of Covenant, but by that time, I'd given up hope of being sent somewhere that was halfway decent. I figured that this was the place they sent all the bad kids that no one wanted. In reality, it was nothing of the sort. ISSC was an orphanage, but the people who worked there were very nice. Our social worker introduced us to Mr. Jefferson, the gentleman who ran the entire school. He was a tall, beefy man with a deep commanding voice that was very intimidating. My initial thoughts were that he would undoubtedly be very hard on us, but that was not the case. Mr. Jefferson turned out to be an understanding man who wanted all the children at ISSC to have a good life.

Vic and I were separated shortly after we arrived. As it turned out, the cottages that we lived in grouped the boys together by certain ages. Since Vic was already a teenager, he was sent to a different cottage than mine. I protested loudly when I learned that we would not be together. As far as I was concerned, my brother was my one and only ally. My previous school had proven that I didn't make friends well, and I didn't relish the idea of being alone with a group of strangers who would probably make fun of me. But that was yet another decision that I had no control over.

For the most part, I kept to myself those first few days. Without Vic to talk to, I felt extremely lost. As best as I could tell, the other boys had been there for quite some time. They were all very familiar with one another, and I didn't think there was anything that I had in common with them.

A week after our arrival, a boy named Joshua approached me and asked if I wanted to go with them to the rec center. l was inclined to say no, but by then I was so lonely that I decided to take him up on his offer.

Before I knew it, I was friendly with most of the thirteen boys who shared the cottage with me. By *friendly* I mean that I was at least invited to play the games they played, and they didn't treat me like a complete outcast. I still wasn't much of a talker. My stutter had been in hiding, but I knew it wasn't completely gone. I worried constantly that if I got too nervous while I was talking, it would act up. I didn't want any of the other boys to hear it, didn't want to give them a reason to tease me.

I saw Vic during meals and when we spent time in the rec room. He seemed to have made a lot of friends, and though he didn't ignore me, I didn't feel as close to him as I once had.

School was still one of my least favorite places. My teachers often commented that I needed to participate more. Participation meant raising my hand and asking questions, and that was something I didn't like to do. It drew too much attention to me, and I preferred to be left in obscurity. One teacher in particular constantly questioned why I was such a withdrawn child. My answer to that was a shrug off my shoulders and a blank stare. How could I possibly explain to her that most of my life had been spent being invisible? I didn't trust the spotlight. Overall, life for my brother and me had been significantly better since we'd arrived at ISSC. The adults who worked there were nice to us. Even though we had to do homework and chores every day, we weren't treated like workhorses and were allowed to have fun. It had turned out to be the best place for Vic and me so far.

Things changed even more for me late during my junior year. Though most of the time I continued to be a loner, I developed a friendship with a boy named Knick. Knick was in a couple of my classes and quite a talker. In fact, he talked enough for the both of us. He was a lot of fun and didn't seem to mind that I didn't say much. We hung out on the weekends, sometimes going to the store for a soda or to a movie. "Hey, Ronnie, you want to go on a date Saturday?" I looked at him strangely. Knick and I had been going to the movies almost every Saturday for months, but over the past few weeks he had been going out with a girl name Barbara. When he'd asked me to wait for him after school, I had hoped it was because he wanted to hang out, not to drag me out with him and his girlfriend.

I shook my head. "No, thanks," I said.

"Oh, come on. Barbara has a sister that wants to meet you." Meet me? Was he kidding? I gave him another strange look. I barely talked to anybody at school. I wondered what in the world made him think I would be able to spend an evening making conversation with a girl. That would be simply impossible.

"No, Knick, that's okay. I don't really want to." For thirty minutes we went back and forth on the subject. Knick was trying his best to convince me while I continued to decline the offer. Eventually, he wore me down, and I finally agreed. As soon as I said yes, I wanted to change my answer, but Knick wouldn't hear it. It was Friday afternoon, and I was left to sweat over this decision all night and well into Saturday. Knick and I arrived at the Huber's' home at six o'clock sharp. Knack's girlfriend, Barbara, opened the door.

"Hi, guys. Come on in," she said warmly. "Good to see you, Ronnie," she said with a smile.

"Hi." I looked nervously around the room.

Mr. and Mrs. Huber were sitting in the living room and greeted Knick when he came in before me. "This is my friend Ronnie," he said, introducing me. Both the adults shook my hand and gave me friendly smiles. I relaxed a little but not much. I still hadn't met Barbara's sister.

"Please have a seat," said Mrs. Huber. "Would you like something to drink?"

"No, ma'am," I answered. My palms started sweating, and I wiped them nervously on my pants.

"You must be Ronnie," said a pretty, brown-haired girl as she walked into the living room. "I'm April." I jumped to my feet. I said hi, and she sat down next to me. We all talked for a few minutes. The Huber's asked me a lot of questions about school, my brother, and the things that I was interested in. It felt a little strange for me. I'd never met any adults who spent that much time listening to kids. I kept my answers short, not wanting to say too much. My past was one that was better kept to myself. I didn't want to tell about all the terrible things that had happened to Vic and me.

"We'd better go," said Barbara, looking at her watch.

"Have a good time, kids," said Mr. Huber. He patted me on the back as he walked us to the door. "Come and visit us again, Ronnie."

"Yes, sir," I mumbled. I doubted that I would go back. Even though being around that family had been nice, I didn't want to get too comfortable. I was too shy when it came to having so much conversation, and I feared that if I stayed too quiet, I'd appear rude. The four of us walked to the movie theater in twos. Knick and Barbara walked a few feet ahead of April and me and talked nonstop. I wasn't sure what to say, but April kept up the conversation, and we managed to talk a little. Nevertheless, I was relieved when we settled into the theater seats and the lights went down. I had at least an hour in which I wouldn't be expected to say anything. I was used to doing that. The night at the movies came and went. Much to my surprise, my initial decision to stay away from the Huber's' house didn't stand. Knick informed me that Mrs. Huber had invited me to have dinner with them the following week, and I accepted. During dinner, the warmth and harmony at the table made me feel good. The family was so easygoing and kind to one another that I couldn't help but soak it all in like a sponge.

April and I got along really well. The two of us had figured out after that first trip to the movies that, while we were very friendly with each other, neither of us was interested in being boyfriend and girlfriend. Once we'd established that, subsequent outings to the movies and to the drugstore for sodas were much more comfortable.

Though my life experiences were limited, the Huber's were unlike any parents I'd even imagined. They were patient and understanding, and they took a real interest in what all of their kids had to say. They even extended that patience and interest to me. Before long, I began to look forward to my visits there. All of the kids treated me as if I belonged, and that was a feeling that I had never had. Their acceptance was the most precious thing I had ever received.

In the days that preceded my eighteenth birthday, I was in a frenzy trying to figure out what I would do for the rest of my life. The policy at ISSC was that children could no longer stay there once they'd reached the age of eighteen. Vic had been required to leave the year before, and I was faced with the same dilemma. To say the least, I was very worried about where I would go and even what would become of me. I had limited work experience and not very much money saved. Even though I spent practically every free moment I had at the Huber's, they weren't my family, and I didn't dare think of imposing on them. I didn't have any other family to speak of. In short, things were looking extremely bleak.

Just when I was beginning to think that I would end up out on the street, the answer came to me. Our last days of school were upon us, and several military recruiters came and visited our class, trying to persuade us to join. When the Army recruiter came and explained the benefits of service, I decided it was the best option for me. It solved my issues of residency and finances all in one shot. The added aspect of being able to travel also intrigued me. A few days before graduation, I signed on the dotted line, and a week later I was sworn in.

On my last night before basic training, the Huber's threw me a surprise going-away party. Knick, whom I considered my best friend, was in on the little secret. He and Barbara were going out and had managed to drag me on yet another of their dates, only this time it was a decoy. Halfway to the theater, Barbara pretended to feel sick, and we turned around to go back to her house. When I stepped over the threshold, the entire family, as well as some of our friends from school, jumped out and yelled, "Surprise!"

To say it was overwhelming is an understatement. I had never been the center of attention for something good before. To see that so many people had come together to see me off made me feel incredible. At the same time, I felt a little sad. I was sure that this was the feeling that I was supposed to have known as a child, and to have been deprived of it for as long as I had hurt tremendously. But I pushed those thoughts aside and enjoyed all that they had planned for me.

We sang songs, played games, and ate plenty of good food. It was late when our friends from school left. I was preparing to leave myself, thinking the party was over. It was then that Mrs. Huber came out with a chocolate cake. Each of the Huber's had a small gift for me, and by then, I had a hard time holding back my tears. David gave me camera to take pictures at my first duty station. April and Charmaine gave me a heavy sweater, and Barbara gave me a scarf. Mr. and Mrs. Huber gave me a small photo album. Inside were pictures of the entire Huber family and some of me and Knick In the back was the one picture that we had all taken together. There was a lump in my throat that made it hard for me to swallow. I looked around the room at all of them.

"Thank you so much," I said quietly.

"You're welcome, Ronnie," Mrs. Huber said, hugging me tightly. "You take care of yourself, and make sure you come back to visit."

"Yes, ma'am. I will."

The rest of the family took turns hugging me. Knick clasped my hand tightly and patted me on the back. "Good luck, buddy," he said.

Mr. Huber drove me back to ISSC that night. Before I got out of the car, he shook my hand again. "If you need anything, you can call us, okay?"

I nodded somberly. For the first time, I actually felt as if there was someone I could call if I had trouble. I got out of the car and watched as Mr. Huber drove away. When I could no longer see the glow of the taillights, I walked back to my cottage.

My bags were already packed, so I slipped out of my clothes and got into bed. I lay awake and thought about the night's events. I was truly going to miss the Huber's, and at that point I almost didn't want to leave. They were like family, and that was what I had always wanted—a family.

# Chapter 16

The bus pulled away from the terminal, and I was on my way to basic training. My stomach pitched with a queasy feeling. I was one of only a few young men who had signed up for the service. Those who had not enlisted had made it their business to try and scare me with horror stories from who knows where. Most of the stories had been so far-fetched that I knew they were false. But then other stories seemed a little more plausible, so I wasn't quite sure what to expect on the day I reported.

Basic training was in Fort Knox, Kentucky. Shortly after my arrival, I found out that it was nothing like the other boys had said. In fact, it wasn't nearly as hard as I imagined it might be. Vic and I had worked harder on the farm. I made a few friends but still tended to keep to myself.

Knick and the Huber's wrote me letters, and I looked forward to mail call each night. They kept me up to date on what was going on with the family. Knick and Barbara were still dating, and he wrote that he was thinking of asking her to marry him. I mused over that thought for a while one night after lights out. It made sense that the two of them would get married. They had dated for quite a while. I wondered what it felt like to want to marry a girl and whether or not I would ever experience it.

After basic training, I headed to South Carolina for my occupational specialty school, field communications. It seemed like an unusual field for me since I was the quiet type, but I found that I was at home behind the radio. I picked up the mechanics of my job quickly and received praise from my instructors for doing well.

Several weeks later, after the completion of my school, I was given ten days leave before leaving for Germany. I had stayed in constant contact with the Huber's, and when I told them about my upcoming time off, they insisted that I come and see them. I accepted immediately. I was looking forward to their warmth and Mrs. Huber's good home cooking.

Things were as if I had never left when I reached their home. We all laughed, talked, and enjoyed one another's company. It still amazed me how much they embraced me into their tight-knit family, but I loved every minute of it. While I was there, Knick and Barbara announced their engagement. I congratulated them, though I wasn't going to be able to make the wedding.

They seemed so happy, and for that matter, so did I. I dreaded the inevitable day that I had to leave these wonderful people behind again.

Wildflecken, Germany, provided sights and sounds that were truly amazing. Having lived on a farm for most of my life, the bustle of city living was a very different experience. During my free time, I wandered the city, taking in the activity. In the evenings, I would write letters to the Huber's and send pictures of all the things I saw. When the holidays came, I made sure to include a few trinkets for each of them.

I continued to do my job as a field radio technician and was in my third year overseas when Barbara and Knick paid me a visit. I played tour guide, showing them around all the popular spots and the beautiful landmarks. Though I had some friends in the area, it was wonderful to see their familiar faces and catch up on what was going on. It was on the last night of their visit while we were at dinner that they dropped some shocking news.

"Ronnie," began Barbara, "ever since Knick first brought you to the house, the whole family has grown attached to you. You've become a part of us that could never be replaced." I looked down into my salad, afraid that my emotions would get away from me. Only in my imagination had I dared to think that the Huber's felt as strongly for me as I did for them. Hearing Barbara say it struck a chord deep in me. I was so caught up in my musings that I completely missed her next statement.

"Ronnie? Did you hear me?"

"Huh?" I looked up again. She was smiling at me and patiently waiting for an answer to her question. The only problem was that I had no idea what her question had been. I looked at Knick for help, but he only smiled. "I'm sorry," I said, feeling a little flustered. "I didn't hear your question."

Barbara laughed. "For a minute I thought you were going to say no." She put her hand over mine to make sure she had my attention. "I said that the whole family has talked it over, and we'd like you to be our brother." It was my turn to laugh.

"Well, I already am, Barbara. You all have been like family to me. You should know that."

"Yes, but we don't want to be *like* family. We want to make it official." Make it official? My head started swimming. I didn't want to ask what she meant. Actually, I couldn't ask. My voice had temporarily been lost. "Mom and Dad want to adopt you. We want you in the family. What do you say?" Years of feeling unwanted, unloved, and worthless fell off of my heart like dead weight.

The thing I wanted most was dangling in front of me. I grinned and nodded my head. "That would be great! I would like that very much."

That night when we returned to Knick and Barbara's hotel, we called the rest of the family. Their rejoicing over the phone was like music to my ears. I didn't know why they'd chosen me, but I was so glad they did.

Months passed before I was able to go to back to the States. By the time I took leave, I had been given orders and was scheduled to report to Vietnam. There was no better time to be with the people I cared for most. They gave me a homecoming that was what I had come to expect from them. The following day, we all went down to the courthouse in Bloomington, Illinois.

Mr. and Mrs. Huber had already filed the necessary paperwork, so I was only required to sign a few documents, and it was a done deal. Though the process was simple and quick, the magnitude of the feeling that came from signing those few papers was tremendous. My heart swelled with pride and a deep sense of love and gratitude. I was part of a family, and it felt wonderful!

# Chapter 17

I pray that you who are going through very painful times will learn to believe in yourselves. It doesn't matter what anyone may ever say about you, you need to know and believe that you are unique and a wonderfully made individual. While no person, especially a child, should have to endure the pain and sadness that you may feel, know that inside, you are stronger than anything you may face. With God's help, you will only grow stronger. Learn to let go of the past, and take hold of God's hand. You can be anything you want to be as long as you believe in yourself. I believe in you, and I salute you, the unwanted child.

I was seventeen when I realized that if I didn't take control of my life, I was going to end up on a path of destruction that would inevitably cause the rest of my life to be as miserable as my childhood had been. The first step in taking control of my life was probably the hardest one I had to take. This was not only because taking the first step of almost anything is difficult but also because that first step required me to forgive. I had begun to know God at that time in my life, and the common theme that resounded in my head as I studied the Bible was forgiveness. I remember being stuck on that word for quite some time. I had had some horrendous experiences in my short life, none of which I felt I could forgive and all of which I knew I would ever forget. Still, the course of my life had been so awful, what did I have to lose?

# Chapter 18

When I took the time to examine all that had transpired in my life, I realized that I was not responsible for the bad that had happened to me. I had no control over those things. I also realized that all of those experiences had left deep scars on my soul and in my heart. I had been abandoned, hurt, deceived, and abused so much that my self-esteem was shot and my faith in others was almost nil. After all, if I had not been able to trust my own parents and those who were caretakers over me, why on earth would I believe in a stranger?

And so it was from that place that I began my new journey in life. Muddled in confusion, riddled with doubt, and not very hopeful, I decided to give love a try. We live and then we die! Sounds simple, doesn't it? But it is not so simple. It is what we do with our lives between those times that really matters. It seems like a long time when we are young, but as we get older time seems to speed up. As we start looking back, we see all the time that we wasted away and all the negative things we did for which we wish we could go back in time and change. But we realize that it is an impossible task. All we can do about those mistakes is learn from them and hope that those we have hurt will forgive us. On the positive side, we can look back and see what we have done to make the world a better place. The trick is to do more to help the world not just for our own sake but for everyone's. We do not know for sure what happens to our spirits when we leave this place. Some say we go to heaven, some say we go to hell, some say we are reincarnated, and some say we stay in limbo. No matter what happens, it surely depends on what we do while we are here.

I have forgiven those who have hurt me. Because of this, I have been able to find what real love is through God, my wife, and my son. When I reached the age of seventeen, I realized that if I did not take control of my life and put it in God's hands, I would be heading for disaster. I immediately told myself that I had no control over what happened to me in my past, but what happened to me from that point on would be my responsibility. I would be making the decisions, right or wrong, and I would have to take the blame for what I did wrong and the credit for what I did right. The decisions would be my own. What I didn't realize was that my past had left many scars buried deep within me, plus I was entering the real world without the knowledge of what it was like to be loved or love someone else. I was always considered a loner. I would turn red every time a girl would talk to me, and I would turn even deeper red if they would mention that my facing was turning red. I made some friends in my cottage at the ISSC home, but since I had been burned so many times before by others, I couldn't allow anyone else to get close to me. I knew that, no matter who they were, they would leave me sooner or later. I felt that I was causing people to leave. After all, from the earliest time I could remember and at every place I lived, after a short time, I was moved to another place. I had no self-esteem or confidence in myself.

# Chapter 19

I was lucky and passed the military exam, and I spent the next twenty years in the Army, being stationed in Europe and Vietnam. I was also able to complete most of my college courses, earning a master's in child welfare and a PhD in social and behavioral science.

In going through my whole life story about being in the child welfare system, because I wanted you to understand that I do know what it's like and why I started doing research on the system. I was hoping that the system had gotten better for us unwanted children.

My results were not happy ones. I found that more than 50 percent of those children's homes have been closed down and that many of the children who were not able to be adopted out or placed with a loving family will have to spend their entire childhoods in the foster care system. More than five hundred thousand children enter the child welfare system every year, and at least 25 percent of them will have to spend their lives in the system until they are eighteen.

I could quote you the statics on the history of the child welfare system, but I feel it would be better if you went to the source, which is the website of the US Department of Health and Human Services.

After reading all these facts, I still believe that children's homes would be better places for these unwanted children. My recommendations are to bring back the children's homes so that these children can be brought up in stable environments where they will have appropriate care. There, they will be able to relate to one another since many of them have gone through similar experiences. They will have immediate medical care. There will be cottage parents who will have time to help them through their pressing problems, and if the cottage parents are not able to help resolve their issues, there will be a social worker and a psychologist on hand to assist them.

"It is time for a call to action"

These children who have been let down by so many deserve a Government that will hold them up to a better standard so these children will have a deserving chance for a better life and will be able to contribute to a better society. Give these children a chance.